Praise for

THE NEW
COLD WAR

'There's a pressing need to put the contest between the US and China into its global context. Robin Niblett does precisely that in *The New Cold War*, showing how today's geopolitical competition is upending international diplomacy, re-shaping multilateral institutions and challenging prospects for a more sustainable world. This is an illuminating book for the interested citizen as well as for those making policy' **Hillary Rodham Clinton, former US Senator and Secretary of State**

'An important, crystal-clear account of contemporary global geopolitics – by one of the UK's leading strategic thinkers. Essential reading' **Peter Frankopan, author of** *The Earth Transformed*

'For those seeking to get their heads round the biggest geopolitical challenges of our time, and especially the developing conflict between China and the liberal democracies, this is an excellent short guide: concise, informed and full of insight' **Sir Lawrence Freedman, author of** *Ukraine and the Art of Strategy*

'In this timely book, Robin Niblett unveils the changing balance of power between the US and China and how it is re-defining international relations. Its clarity makes it essential reading, above all for Europeans seeking to chart a course to defend their interests and values' **Arancha González, Dean, Paris School of International Affairs at Sciences Po and former Foreign Minister of Spain**

THE NEW COLD WAR

HOW THE CONTEST BETWEEN THE US AND CHINA WILL SHAPE OUR CENTURY

Robin Niblett

Atlantic Books
London

First published in Great Britain in 2024 by Atlantic Books,
an imprint of Atlantic Books Ltd.

10 9 8 7 6

A CIP catalogue record for this book is available from the
British Library.

Trade Paperback ISBN: 978 1 80546 211 8
E-book ISBN: 978 1 80546 212 5

Printed in Great Britain by TJ Books Ltd, Padstow, Cornwall

Atlantic Books
An imprint of Atlantic Books Ltd
Ormond House
26–27 Boswell Street
London
WC1N 3JZ

www.atlantic-books.co.uk

Contents

Introduction

On 1 February 2023, Chase Doak, editor of the *Billings Gazette*, was scanning the clear blue sky above Billings, Montana, when he spotted a strange white dot, hanging there, stationary, like a daytime star. With the help of the *Gazette* photographer's long-range camera, he saw it was a balloon. This giant descendant of its nineteenth-century forebears had been kitted out by China's People's Liberation Army (PLA) with a twenty-first-century payload of technology and a solar power array the size of three school buses. It was a shocking apparition, even though it posed no threat to people on the ground and, as a tool for aerial surveillance and signals intelligence, its impact was hotly debated.[1]

Nevertheless, the sheer brazenness of its intrusion over the American Midwest, near silos of the country's arsenal of land-based intercontinental nuclear missiles, triggered a volcanic reaction in the US Congress. Republicans accused the Biden administration of failing to defend US skies. Democrats decried a deeply hostile act by America's communist rival, despite the likelihood that the balloon had simply veered off course. By 4 February, once it had drifted over the South Carolina coast, President Biden ordered the slow-moving and defenceless intruder be shot down – by an F-22 fighter capable of flying at nearly two and a half times the speed of sound and hitting targets over 150 nautical miles away. The brutal mismatch of power provided a convenient distraction in Beijing from the embarrassment of the balloon's discovery. The *Global Times*, mouthpiece of the Chinese Communist Party (CCP), wrote that it was like 'shooting a mosquito with a cannon'.[2]

The 'balloon incident' exposed for all the toxic state of US–China relations and the deep anxieties on both sides. US and Chinese governments have long engaged in aerial surveillance, but mostly through satellites in invisible geostationary orbit, or through equally invisible digital penetration of each other's databases and national security infrastructure. It took the balloon, and the subsequent revelation that it was far from the first to traverse the US and its allies in the Asia–Pacific, to awaken US citizens to the scale of the growing contest.

It also served as a reminder of the ambiguities that riddle the relationship. Once the downed balloon was pulled to the surface off Myrtle Beach and the entrails of its payload dissected, they were found to contain US dual-use chips and other components; just as dismantling the F-22 that shot down the balloon would likely reveal Chinese-sourced micro-electronics and rare earth minerals buried inside its avionics and missiles.[3] This is hardly surprising. After China's entry into the World Trade Organization (WTO) in 2001, US–China economic relations grew exponentially. Chinese companies supplied American consumers with well-produced and low-priced everyday goods and US companies with low-value but essential components. US companies supplied China with iPhones, computers and advanced semiconductors, as well as food and fuels. And both sides invested in each other's economies, from established companies to start-ups.

But within ten years, political relations had begun to deteriorate, especially after the rise to power in 2012 of the more authoritarian and externally assertive CCP General Secretary Xi Jinping. Leaders in Washington and allied capitals in Europe and the Asia–Pacific have come to the realization that China's growing economic power has translated into greater capacity for the CCP to quash any dissent or possibility of political pluralism inside China. And that they have been helping China on its journey to greater military-technical self-sufficiency, which in turn is empowering China to challenge them abroad. Since 2013, there has been a growing catalogue of near misses between Chinese and US aircraft and naval vessels patrolling the contested skies and seas around Taiwan and Southeast Asia. Any one of them could have easily resulted in deaths of servicemen and a far more dangerous fallout than from the balloon incident.

The last ten years have ripped the veil from the notion that closer economic relations between the US and China could be insulated from these growing political tensions. The hope was that, unlike the US and the Soviet Union, the US and China could each grow stronger together. Instead, they have slipped into what was first termed in 1951, four years after the start of the last Cold War, as the 'security dilemma', whereby the actions by one side to increase its security engenders new insecurity and counter-reactions in the other, pulling both into an inescapable vortex towards war.[4] Four-star General Mike Minihan, head of the US Air Mobility Command, even warned in a memo in January 2023 that the US and China are on course to 'fight' over Taiwan in 2025. He is not the only senior member of the US military to have issued such warnings in recent years.[5]

Descent into the antagonistic, destructive rivalry that characterized the last Cold War could possibly be avoided by regular consultations, channels for crisis communications, and by agreements for military de-escalation and transparency. But the problem is that these two countries are on opposite sides of a profound and open-ended global competition between two political systems that are incompatible and mutually hostile.

As the Director of Chatham House for fifteen years, I travelled regularly to China to speak at conferences on international relations. I was always struck by my Chinese counterparts' obsession with understanding the drivers of what they called today's 'great power competition'. Drawing on historical experience and the writing of American theorists of international relations, they believed they understood the central reason for US and Chinese competition: the rise of a new great power would inevitably be blocked by the existing great power, leading to what US academic Graham Allison first described in 2012 as the 'Thucydides trap', named after the Athenian general who wrote about the causes of the First Peloponnesian War in the late fourth century BC. Allison equates the US with Sparta, trying to resist the rise of China (Athens in Thucydides' day), even if this leads to conflict.[6]

The solution, according to my Chinese interlocutors, was for China to demonstrate that it does not want to replace the US as the world's dominant power, and for the US to accept China's rise as its equal globally as well as in Asia. This would allow the two sides to co-exist peacefully and avoid a repetition of the world wars in the first half of the twentieth century, or of the Cold War in its latter half.

But I argued that they were missing the point. Sure, the security dilemma between the US and China could possibly be attenuated by confidence-building measures and negotiated frameworks for economic cooperation and competition. But we need to recognize that the conflict between the two sides is also ideological. It is rooted in the fear that the leaders of two very different political systems have of the other. The single-party system represented by the CCP rejects any internal challenge to state power, while the liberal democratic system championed by the US places checks and balances on state power, and the rights of the individual are at its centre. The United States and China have different visions not only for the best form of domestic governance, but also for international order. Both want their system to dominate the twenty-first century.

This is why they are now engaged in a contest that is global and unbridgeable. Why we have entered a new Cold War and are no longer just in its foothills.[7] Why this Cold War's tinderbox is Taiwan, a democratic outpost next to the communist behemoth. Why its two protagonists are working so hard to draw allies and friends to their side from across the world, especially countries outside the northern hemisphere that together constitute what is now called the Global South. And it is why the contest encompasses all major instruments of statecraft: diplomacy, technology, military power, intelligence, foreign aid, culture and, critically, trade and investment. After all, if two well-matched and nuclear-armed powers are involved in such deeply rooted rivalry, then the battle for economic and technological supremacy will be paramount, and companies will be on the front line, whether they like it or not.

We stand at the very beginning of the New Cold War, with no sense of how or when it will end. Russian President Vladimir Putin's rash decision to undertake a full-scale invasion of Ukraine on 24 February 2022, and Xi's decision to remain faithful to the spirit of the declaration that he signed with Putin just before the invasion stating there are 'no limits' to the friendship between the two states, have welded China to Russia in a conflict with no discernible solution.[8] It has also knitted America and its European and Pacific allies together in opposition. The March 2023 agreement between the United States, Australia and the United Kingdom to develop cutting-edge dual-use technologies, including a new fleet of Australian nuclear-powered sub-marines to patrol the Pacific, measures its milestones in decades, not years.[9] Meanwhile, President Xi has set 2049 as the target for China to complete its process of national 'rejuvenation' and to overcome America's policy of 'all-round containment, encirclement and suppression'.[10]

But the New Cold War will be nothing like the last one between the Soviet Union and the West, which ran through to 1990 and defined the second half of the twentieth century. Its geographic shape and internal dynamics are different, which can offer us hope for the future. Above all, its two sides have travelled far down the road of economic integration. Unless there is a cataclysmic event, a complete U-turn is impossible for both. Instead, they are reversing carefully into the New Cold War, trying not to sever all their connections and hoping that, once they have backed away from each other far enough, they can map a new route that will sustain some of the mutual benefits they enjoyed over the last twenty-plus years.

Understanding this and the other main differences between the two Cold Wars is an essential prerequisite for avoiding an accidental or conscious transition into a globally devastating hot war. This book asks: how is China different from the Soviet Union? How is the US of the twenty-first century different from that of the late twentieth? What are the priorities of countries in the Global South, and which international institutions will be most effective in a more divided world? Answering these questions matters if the two sides are still to cooperate on shared global challenges, and if the world's liberal democracies are to design a strat-egy for the New Cold War that enables them to defend their freedoms as successfully this time as the last.

With this goal in mind, the book also lays out five rules to manage the risks inherent in the early stages of the New Cold War and prevent a complete breakdown in US–China relations. They offer the possibility that when it finally ends, more countries and peoples will have embraced the freedoms enshrined in democratic systems of governance than do today.

1

China is no Soviet Union

Understanding the differences between China today and the Soviet Union during the last Cold War is a good place to start when assessing the main differences between the geopolitical contest that defined the second half of the twentieth century and the one that will define the first half, at least, of the twenty-first. As the Soviet Union did before, China today constitutes the dominant magnetic pole of a form of government and international outlook that is the rival of the community of states, led by the United States, that define themselves as liberal democracies. But, as we shall see, China poses a more significant structural challenge to the US and its allies than did the Soviet Union. Why? Because China is still at the beginning of marshalling its growing power to the service of its foreign policies, and its sources of power are more extensive and diverse than those of the Soviet Union.

The inherent limits of Soviet power

The Soviet Union's elevated position in international affairs after 1945 had much to do with its role as one of the main two victors, alongside the United States, at the end of the Second World War. By most measures, the USSR reached its relative peak during the first decade of the first Cold War. In December 1945, it occupied all central and eastern Europe and, by 1948, had engineered communist party rule throughout the region, with most governments indirectly controlled from Moscow. These countries then came together along with the Soviet Union in 1955 under the umbrella of the Warsaw Pact, a military alliance led by Moscow and supposedly designed to protect its members from attack by the US-led NATO alliance. The Warsaw Pact and its economic counterpart, Comecon, provided the Soviet Union with a large geographic buffer to its west, from which the principal invasions and threats to its territorial integrity had emanated for the previous five centuries. And they gave the Soviet Union an economic and strategic weight well beyond its own intrinsic human and material resources.

The Soviet Union's role as a permanent member of the United Nations Security Council and as a leading nuclear-armed state also enhanced its security and global standing. And its self-sufficiency in natural resources – especially oil, gas, coal and food – added to its ability to follow an autarkic path, much like the US had done until it was drawn into Europe's two major wars. But as former US National Security Advisor Zbigniew Brzezinski presciently wrote in 1986, 'the Soviet Union is like a giant with steel hands but rotten innards. It can crush in its grip weaker opponents but a spreading corrosion is eating away at its system.'[1] Its centrally planned economy was unable to match the technological innovations and gains in productivity in the United States and Europe.

Between 1973 and 1990, Soviet GDP per capita grew from approximately $6,000 to a little under $10,000, while that in the US grew from $16,600 to $23,300, leaving the USSR stuck at a ratio of 35 per cent of the US level over this period, despite having a population 16 per cent larger than that of the US (290 million to the US's 250 million in 1990).[2] To try to sustain its competitive position in relation to an ever more technologically dynamic United States, the Soviet leadership concluded that it needed to transform its economic model. But Mikhail Gorbachev's programmes of *glasnost* (openness and transparency) and *perestroika* (economic restructuring) instead ended up exposing the depth of the Soviet Union's weakness and its tenuous hold over its satellites. After the collapse of communist governments in central Europe and of the Warsaw Pact in 1989–90, the subsequent implosion of the Soviet Union through 1991 led to the fledging of fourteen independent states around Russia's periphery, and Russia's retreat into a still geographically vast but much smaller country of some 140 million people.[3]

China is still starting its journey as a superpower

China's gestation as a great power following the end of the Second World War has been more difficult and convoluted. On paper, despite the huge loss of civilian and military lives, second only to that of the Soviet Union, China was also one of the winners in 1945. But the subsequent civil war between the nationalist Kuomintang (KMT) and the communists led by Mao Zedong meant that the People's Republic of China did not come into being until 1949. And, with US support, the anti-communist KMT held on to China's seat at the UN, as well as the island of Taiwan, to which its leadership decamped after their defeat, creating a separate political entity and the tinderbox for the New Cold War seventy years later.

That China has taken so long to reach superpower status is a reminder that Mao's chaotic rule – which included the devastating Great Leap Forward in 1958–60 and the violent and tumultuous Cultural Revolution from 1966–76 – held

China back, even as he cemented the country's sovereignty and independence after nearly 200 years of foreign intervention. In 1980, China had the largest population in the world, but its GDP per capita averaged only $195. Compare this to Mexico, also a newly industrializing economy at that time, where the GDP per capita was $3,000.[4]

It is also a reminder that, unlike the Soviet Union, which began the last Cold War protected by a ring of allied, buffer states, China has none. Instead, the Chinese Communist Party (CCP) has spent much of the last seventy years consolidating control over China's periphery, from Tibet to Hong Kong and Xinjiang, and defending its external borders, often through conflict, as in the case of the Korean War (in 1952) and the wars with India (in 1962 and 1967) and their continuing border skirmishes. Today, the CCP is trying to assert control over islands and waters in the South China Sea that it claims are part of its sovereign territory. And it is intensely focused on ending Taiwan's political separation from the mainland.

Unlike the Soviet Union, therefore, which imploded just some forty years after achieving superpower status, China is still near the beginning of a much slower journey to being a leading world power. In 2023, China's 1.4 billion people accounted for nearly 18 per cent of the world's total, five times as large as the Soviet Union at the time of its collapse, and ten times as large as Russia's and four times as large as America's today. And yet, China's GDP per capita still averaged only $12,500, a fifth of America's, and this figure conceals vast differences in wealth: those in rural and inland areas had average disposable incomes of about a fifth of those in the wealthier coastal areas, and over 35 per cent of workers, nearly 300 million, live precariously as internal migrants.[5]

China started its run of consistent GDP growth only after 1980, when Mao's successor, Deng Xiaoping, launched his policy of market opening along with an emphasis on mass education and urbanization. Nevertheless, after four decades of almost uninterrupted growth, China's GDP is close to overtaking America's in gross terms. And in certain, more qualitative domains, China is well on its way to matching or even surpassing the US and Europe.

Gone are the days when China was the sweatshop to the world. Its education system trains almost all Chinese to a high standard, and its universities are currently producing each year between two and four million graduates in science, technology and engineering.[6] China has achieved revolutionary breakthroughs in cutting-edge areas of high technology, such as quantum computing and building the world's most powerful supercomputer, and now matches Germany in many areas of advanced manufacturing. Leveraging its enormous domestic market, China is also the only country apart from the US to have constructed its own large-scale digital companies, combining mobile and online payments platforms such as Alipay alongside multi-service digital providers such as WeChat. With ready access to the private data of over a billion citizens, China stands at the forefront of breakthroughs in artificial intelligence applications, from speech and image recognition to self-driving cars.[7]

In other areas, however, the Chinese economy continues to operate, at best, at the level of an emerging market or, sometimes, of a developing economy. Obstacles to growth include still immature capital markets; over-reliance on the property sector and construction as a motor for growth; under-developed social welfare programmes, whether in health, education or pensions; and a rapidly ageing society. In January 2023, the National Bureau of Statistics reported that there were 850,000 fewer Chinese at the end of 2022 than there were at the start, raising the fearful prospect that China will grow old before it grows rich.[8] The lack of a reliable social safety net drives most young Chinese to save anywhere between 30 and 50 per cent of their monthly income, which, in turn, puts a cap on private consumption as a generator of growth.[9] Young Chinese have also emerged from the shock and stress of the COVID lockdowns rejecting the workaholic lives of their parents. On social media, they celebrate the heretical ideas of 'lying flat', rather than working from nine to nine for six days a week, or 'letting it rot', which implies not bothering to work at all.[10]

Making sure China stays safe in the world

China's course is set by a small cadre at the apex of the CCP and, whatever their differences over tactics, they generally avoid the frequent shifts in direction that are the hallmarks of an openly competitive democratic process. What then are their priorities as they map out the country's future and the journey to arrive there?

President Xi Jinping has stated that, by 2049, the centenary of the founding of the People's Republic of China, the country should have regained its place at the apex of the world, where it stood, as the largest country in terms of economic capacity, for several centuries during the second millennium, until the West launched its Industrial Revolution early in the nineteenth century.[11] China's rejuvenation should also involve major improvements in the living standards of the majority of Chinese citizens, thereby ensuring the CCP's continued legitimacy at the helm of the country.

Unlike the USSR, China could prove successful in achieving its goal. Given the sheer size of its population and economic output, China has the potential to outmatch the old Soviet Union at its height and usurp America's position at the top of the superpower ladder. But, despite delivering consistently high levels of economic growth since the mid-1980s, China's decline in the early nineteenth century and a hundred years of humiliation at the hands of occupying European powers and Japan between 1840 and 1945 has left deep scars among the CCP leadership, as well as the Chinese people.[12] As recently as March 2023, Xi bitterly complained that, 'bullying by foreign powers and frequent wars tore the country apart and plunged the Chinese people into an abyss of great suffering'.[13] The fear of external interference and internal chaos that would undermine China's journey to national rejuvenation is profound.

Two elements lie at the core of their concern. The first is that the United States, which has been the dominant power in the Asia–Pacific region since the end of the Second World War, will block China's rise. Responding to this risk lies at the heart of China's two-decade long investment in its armed forces. Having relied on the People's Liberation Army to protect its land borders since 1949, the CCP has invested its ever-growing military budget into building what is now the world's largest navy, even though it possesses only three aircraft carriers so far to America's eleven. And, after contenting itself with a minimum nuclear deterrent force of 200 nuclear warheads for several decades, China is now racing to match the US and Russia, which each have some 1,500 warheads deployed, and could have over 1,000 operational warheads by 2030.[14]

Importantly, China is also building its asymmetric strength, in other words its capacity to negate America's qualitative military superiority through alternative means. The best example is its early development of hypersonic anti-ship missiles, which can travel at five times the speed of sound, making them more difficult to intercept. US naval forces in the South China Sea and Taiwan Strait, two areas where the US contests China's territorial claims, are now more vulnerable to attack. China also shocked the US in August 2021 with the successful test of the first ever 'hypersonic glide vehicle', which detached from a ballistic missile and circled the globe before reaching its target.[15] The message was clear – Washington cannot count on its anti-ballistic missile systems to protect their forward-deployed forces based around China, from Guam to Japan. In many other areas of defence-related high technology – such as supercomputers and AI, drone 'swarms', cyber warfare and anti-satellite systems – China already either matches or outmatches the US.[16]

But the CCP's sense of strategic vulnerability does not originate only from historical experience and the size of the national territory and seas it must protect against the US and others. Whereas the Soviet Union rose to superpower status partly on the back of its massive natural resource endowments, China is dependent on commodity imports to feed its growing economy. It currently imports over 70 per cent of its oil, nearly 50 per cent of its gas, and over 70 per cent of its iron ore.[17] Ensuring the future security of these supplies is a primary motivator for Beijing's investments in its navy, for its strategy of taking control of the South China Sea, and for wanting to draw Taiwan back into the fold as quickly as possible. If it fails, China's security will continue to be hostage to the goodwill of the US and its regional allies – Japan, South Korea, Taiwan and the Philippines – that constitute the 'first island chain' of US bases and basing agreements strung along China's coast.

Overcoming China's lack of natural resources also lies at the heart of the CCP's foreign policy. The Chinese government has assiduously developed its power and influence in resource-rich and strategically located countries far beyond its immediate periphery, which are critical to ensuring its access to stable supplies of natural resources in the future. Since Xi Jinping announced the launch of the 'Belt and Road Initiative' in 2013, China has signed a plethora of bilateral agreements and invested up to $1 trillion to help develop physical infrastructure in countries that connect it with those supplies – above all in Africa, Central Asia and Latin America.[18] China has also constructed a so-called 'string of pearls', a series of port facilities from Gwadar on Pakistan's coast with the Arabian Sea, to Djibouti, near the entrance to the Red Sea, and Hambantota in Sri Lanka. On 4 February 2022, twenty days before Russia's full-scale invasion of Ukraine, China announced its 'no limits partnership' with Russia, which will be an essential source of energy and critical minerals to help feed China's voracious economic appetite. And it played a key role in mediating the resumption in March 2023 of the security agreement between Saudi Arabia and Iran, two of its main suppliers of crude oil.[19]

The nucleus of the first Cold War lay in Europe, where the Soviet Union and Warsaw Pact faced off against the US and NATO. The peripheries of the Soviet–US contest, whether in Cuba and Central America, Vietnam or Angola, were mostly about demonstrating global influence and credibility to their allies, probing for weaknesses, or distracting the other side from the pivotal European theatre of their competition. In contrast, the combination of China's size with its economic vulnerability means that the contest for influence between the US and China will be truly global. And the New Cold War will be played out above all in what is now termed the Global South: in Africa, in Latin America, in the Middle East, and in South and Southeast Asia, all regions where China is challenging America's long-standing position as the leading power situated at the strategic intersections of the world.

Preserving stability at home

The challenges facing China are not only external. Like the Soviet Communist Party, the CCP may appear to possess almost limitless autocratic power, but it still carries within it the DNA of a secret, revolutionary movement, motivated by a profound and instinctive sense of insecurity. With an eye to China's long history, the CCP leadership fears popular upheaval and ethnic separatism in equal measure. With an eye to China's century of humiliation and, more recently, the collapse of communism in the Soviet Union, it believes these are weaknesses that the US can exploit.

A central tenet for the CCP leadership, therefore, is absolute intolerance of political opposition or other form of political contestation – whether from individuals, lawyers, unions or NGOs. Under Xi Jinping, the CCP has tightened even further its control over public information and deployed an iron fist against any form of dissent. It has deployed tens of thousands of officials to man the 'great firewall' that aims to seal the Chinese population from the global internet. And it is constantly experimenting with new forms of digital tracking and surveillance that mix positive protections for citizens from unscrupulous businesses with elaborate programs targeted at monitoring and controlling dissidents and minorities, using tools ranging from DNA databases to facial recognition.[20] For the CCP, political conformity ranks alongside law-abiding behaviour, and it seeks to mould people's behaviour towards the party line through a mix of inducement and punishment.

But the CCP knows that control gets you only so far and will fail unless the party also delivers to the Chinese people the future that they expect. One part of that expectation is that China is becoming great again; that it will be treated with the respect the Chinese people believe their country is due. In this sense, the CCP's ability to reabsorb Taiwan into a greater China is as much a test of the CCP's domestic credibility and legitimacy as of its management of China's security. The other part of the contract between the party and the people is for Chinese citizens to achieve a level of personal wellbeing at least equal to that of other developed nations around the world.

Achieving this second part of the contract lies at the root of one of the most profound differences between this Cold War and the last. The CCP learned an important lesson watching the collapse of the Soviet Union. From Deng Xiaoping onwards, the party's overriding priority has been to accelerate China's economic growth without permitting any challenge to the power of the party. To do so, they have focused their efforts on domestic economic reform, without the parallel process of political opening and transparency that Gorbachev believed was reform's necessary precursor.

This focus on economic reform lay behind the CCP's strategic decision under Deng to abandon economic self-sufficiency and engage with the global economy. Unlike their former Soviet counterparts, CCP leaders have not sought to create a parallel global economic order as a means of buttressing their Marxist–Leninist system at home. To the extent that they have an overarching global economic goal, it is to leverage trade and investment with the rest of the world in order to drive domestic growth and, thereby, to protect the party from external or internal subversion.

Russian leaders, like their Soviet predecessors, perceive global economic integration as a risk to their power and state sovereignty. In contrast, the CCP sees participation in economic globalization as an opportunity to expand its economic strength and political influence. It hopes that, eventually, China's size will enable it to dominate the global economy and thereby further strengthen China's internal security. Unlike the USSR, China can set terms to others, and unlike the US and its allies, its centralized political system allows it to pursue national economic goals more consistently.

However, the CCP continues to want to control the extent of the country's engagement in economic globalization. This is why it limits foreign investment in sensitive economic sectors; why it has reasserted a central role for state-owned enterprises in critical sectors; why the People's Bank of China has still not lifted capital controls and enabled the full internationalization of the renminbi (RMB), the Chinese currency. This instinct to control can be a weakness – as the CCP discovered when over-stimulus in 2009–14 led to runaway urban construction and a boom and bust in the property sector. Chinese companies also made many bad bets internationally as they rolled out Xi Jinping's Belt and Road Initiative, from the bankrupt port of Hambantota in Sri Lanka to the failed railway project linking Kenya and Uganda.[21]

Nevertheless, the extent to which China has changed the global economic context, not only for itself but also for the rest of the world, points to the next fundamental difference between this Cold War and the last. China, the US and its allies have started the twenty-first century intimately, some would say inextricably, interconnected.

2

Reversing into the New Cold War

It is deeply ironic that China's emergence as a global economic power has been facilitated by its arch-rival, the United States, resulting in deep and in some cases perverse economic interconnections that the US never had with the Soviet Union. Both sides have now woken up to the risks of this interdependence and are looking to cut some of the connective tissue that has grown around their relationship. Several of the early signs of a new Cold War reflect these mutual efforts by each country to reset and 'derisk' its relations with the other.

America still at the apex of the global economy, for now

The US, plus its largest post-war allies – Canada, France, Germany, Italy, Japan and the UK, known informally since 1975 as the Group of Seven, or G7 – constituted the world's largest economic force throughout the last Cold War. The US share of world GDP hit its peak in the 1950s, at nearly 30 per cent, when it emerged victorious and largely untouched by the devastation of the Second World War. By

1990 it still accounted for 26.5 per cent, while the now floundering USSR's share was 9 per cent and China's a mere 1.6 per cent. Since then, the US share of global GDP has drifted down only marginally to 25 per cent (2022), while China's share has increased exponentially to nearly 18 per cent and Europe's and Japan's have declined in relative terms.[1]

As America's GDP grew, so did its military power. Just by spending 3–4 per cent of its GDP annually on its armed forces, the US's defence budget grew from $500 billion in 1990 to just under $800 billion in 2023, equal to about 40 per cent of the world's total defence spending that year.[2] Nearly eighty years after the end of the Second World War, the US remains the world's pre-eminent military power. It has military bases and troops stationed from Japan and South Korea, throughout the Pacific and Indian Oceans, to Qatar and Saudi Arabia, as well as those present across Europe as part of the NATO alliance. Economic wealth and military-technical capability are inextricably linked in American minds – and have become so for the Chinese also.

The US economy retains the structural advantages that have enabled it to rise to its position of global economic primacy. It occupies a large, mostly hospitable and sparsely populated land mass and, unlike China, has only two contiguous neighbours – Canada and Mexico – with which it has benign if sometimes complex relations. It is enormously rich in natural resources. The US is the world's largest producer of oil and natural gas, having mastered in the 1980s unconventional techniques, such as hydraulic fracturing and horizontal drilling, to extract new seams of its abundant resources at mass scale since the turn of the millennium. It is also self-sufficient in food production and is one of the world's leading agricultural exporters.

The US has a relatively open market economy, with a light-touch approach to business regulation and strong protections for property rights. The American Dream continues to attract immigrants from all over the world – one million in 2022 alone, taking the foreign-born share of the US population to 46 million, 14 per cent of the total.[3] Their talent, initiative and hard work underpin America's service and manufacturing sectors and often conceive the start-ups like Google and Zoom that generate new economic wealth in high-technology sectors.

The US retains much of the dynamism that has enabled it to sustain its primary economic and geopolitical position. It is the world's leader in high-technology development and innovation, the latest being in AI applications, such as OpenAI's ChatGPT and Google's Bard, that have been trained by large language models. It holds its position by drawing on its global dominance of higher education and research, and its capacity to finance start-ups within a large and wealthy single market of 330 million people. It has the world's largest and most liquid capital markets and benefits massively and uniquely from the dollar's role as the world's dominant reserve currency. The fact that so many governments and institutions believe that investing in the US dollar is the safest way for them to protect the value of their reserves means that the US is the only country that can confidently borrow money internationally in its own currency, a privilege of which it has made full use in the last couple of decades.

There have been many predictions since the late 1980s of America's imminent economic decline.[4] Most of them assume that the drivers will be internal political dysfunctionality or 'imperial overreach', or some combination of both. They have proved wrong – so far. Through the Cold War and the post-Cold War periods, with their hugely costly overseas interventions in Vietnam and Iraq and their financial market crashes, the US has resisted all challenges to its position. There was a moment in the early 1960s, the so-called 'Sputnik moment' after the Soviets beat the Americans to launch the first manned space flight to orbit the Earth, when the US feared it was being overtaken technologically by the USSR; but it was brief. Japan's economic charge in the 1980s and the EU's establishment of its single market and currency since have failed to dislodge the US.

China's rise presents the sternest test yet to US supremacy. And the competition between the two countries, as they jostle for position at the top of the economic and technological ladder, now provides one of the foundational elements of the New Cold War.

China moving to the centre

China has experienced a remarkable economic rise since 2001, when it joined the WTO. Classified as a 'developing economy', China was able to take advantage of low-tariff access for its exports to world markets without having to open its economy to others to the same extent. Nonetheless, greater openness and competition at home, plus an influx of foreign direct investment, new technology and expertise, all coupled with massive, multi-year government spending on domestic infrastructure (property, transport and urbanization) unleashed an economic boom. In 2001, China's GDP stood at $1.2 trillion (to America's $10.25 trillion), whereas in 2022 it hit $18 trillion (to America's $25.9 trillion). In terms of what economists call 'purchasing power parity' – what the Chinese can buy with their money compared to other countries – China's combined GDP at 16.6 per cent of the world total is now higher than that of the US at 15.8 per cent.[5]

China's impact on the world economy has been remarkable and will continue to grow. In 2009, China became the world's largest exporter and is now well ahead of its nearest rivals, the US and Germany.[6] Its exports started with basic manufactured goods, ranging from textiles and toys to furniture. But it has steadily moved up the manufacturing 'value chain' – into high-speed rail systems and pharmaceuticals – and now competes with German, Italian and other Western companies on machine tools, electronic appliances and, most recently, cars. Chinese companies have also become essential component suppliers to manufacturing companies around the world, making them indispensable in most global supply chains.

China is especially competitive in the new green technologies that will power the world in the twenty-first century, having subsidized the sector's development in its protected domestic market. Through the 2010s, China accounted for 90 per cent of global rare earth mining and processing, which are essential for wind turbines, as well as for smartphones and a host of electronic sub-components. By 2023, it produced over 90 per cent of processed lithium and cobalt, the feedstock of the battery technology at the heart of our transition to electric vehicles.[7]

And, because of the vast size and growing wealth of its domestic market, China has become one of the world's leading destinations for others' exports, creating opportunities for economic growth across the world. Countries in Southeast Asia have been among the biggest beneficiaries, seeing their GDP grow collectively from roughly $600 billion in 2000 to $3 trillion in 2020, helped by China's low-cost inputs into their own exports.[8] Now, Chinese companies are investing in manufacturing production across the region as Chinese labour costs rise, helping increase the region's share of global foreign direct investment from 7 per cent in 2011–17 to 12 per cent in 2021 and pushing its total stock of foreign investment to $3.1 trillion.[9]

China is the world's largest import market for global commodities, not only rare minerals, but also iron ore, copper, soya beans and palm oil, creating important inter-dependencies with commodity exporters across the world, from Africa to Latin America. It is also the principal market for the world's two most successful manufacturing export-ers, Japan and Germany. China, not the US or Europe, is now the main destination for Saudi Arabia's oil exports. And China, not the US or Europe, is the largest market for Brazil's agricultural exports. In 2022, China was the main trading partner for 120 countries in the world.[10]

Thanks to the growth of its domestic high-tech sector, China is also offering those emerging markets that can afford it, such as in the Gulf States, the chance to leapfrog reliance on manufacturing and use technology to help drive growth. Chinese companies are working with Saudi Arabia on its massive programme of new city building, led by NEOM that, if all goes according to plan, will emerge, like a mirage from the desert and run for 170 kilometres along the shore of the Red Sea. China will help Saudi Arabia infuse these cities with smart technology solutions for their transport, telecommunications and integrated energy needs, as well as the surveillance technologies that are attractive to governments in the Middle East.[11]

China is forging itself into the first true geo-economic rival to the US since the first half of the twentieth century, when the US displaced the declining British Empire. As President Biden put it in his foreword to the 2022 National Security Strategy, 'The People's Republic of China harbors the intention and, increasingly, the capacity to re-shape the international order into one that tilts the global playing field to its benefit.'[12]

We got it wrong

It would be naive to think that the US should welcome China's rise. On the contrary, the more successful China becomes, the more it feeds US concerns that, perversely, it is enabling its rival's growing power.

In the 1990s and early 2000s, many Americans believed that China's integration into the global economy would go hand in hand with political opening; or that, at the very least, Beijing would buy into the market-based approach that has been the goal of US global economic leadership since the 1950s.[13] When former US Deputy Secretary of State Bob Zoellick challenged China to be 'a responsible stakeholder', he meant, implicitly, that China should accept its membership of a global economic order defined by American principles.[14] For their part, the Chinese leadership hoped the US would accept China's rise out of economic self-interest, irrespective of the two countries' very different economic models and systems of governance and their status as geopolitical competitors. As a result, the two sides allowed their economies to become intertwined. The US is now China's single largest country export market, accounting for over 16 per cent ($583 billion) of its total exports in 2022 (although China's combined exports to the EU are higher, at close to 20 per cent of the total).[15]

Given the role of the US as the largest and most liquid global financial market, the Chinese government has also reinvested half of its hard currency surplus into US Treasuries and other US dollar-denominated assets.[16] Chinese companies chose the New York Stock Exchange as their main venue for overseas capital raising through the 2010s and up to the start of the COVID pandemic in 2020. And China became completely dependent on the US for the advanced semiconductors that power its own high-technology industries, from smartphones to telecommunications infrastructure, and for its ambitious plans to use AI to enhance its economic productivity.[17]

The US trades far more with Canada and Mexico than it does with China, which is its third largest export destination. But China is an important market for some key sectors, including agriculture (principally soybeans, wheat and corn), semiconductors and related components, oil and gas, and pharmaceuticals, which saw US exports grow 38 per cent in 2022.[18] China is projected to have the largest air travel market in the world by 2030 by value, having overtaken the US in total passenger flights in 2022. By 2036, there could be 1.5 billion aviation passengers, nearly a billion more than in 2016 and 50 per cent more than the US.[19] Boeing's success or not in selling into this market will be critical to its future. Exports to China currently support over one million jobs in the US, and several globally competitive US service sectors also see China as central to their own growth plans, including financial services (investment banking, pensions and wealth management, and insurance), and entertainment service providers, from the NBA (National Basketball Association) to Disney.

But rather than perceiving this two-way trade as a 'win–win' proposition, both sides are now racing to disentangle some of their economic interdependencies, as the geopolitically competitive nature of their relationship becomes more apparent. In the 1990s and 2000s, when China was at the start of its journey of economic modernization, the US largely chose to overlook the industrial scale of China's theft of US intellectual property. No longer. As Chinese companies began outcompeting their US counterparts in many high-tech sectors, such as telecommunications and financial technology, the Americans started to hit back. President Obama personally raised the issue of Chinese commercial hacking with Xi Jinping during the latter's visit to Washington in September 2015. But the intrusions soon picked back up, leading both the Trump and Biden administrations to respond with targeted sanctions against named perpetrators.[20]

Similarly, there is little tolerance now that a far wealthier China still insists on being treated as a 'developing economy' under WTO rules and is unwilling to share the benefits of its growth with its trading partners. Between 2018 and 2019, the Trump administration's Trade Representative, Bob Lighthizer, led the process of imposing tariffs of between 7.5 and 25 per cent on $360 billion worth of Chinese exports to the US, arguing that the entrenched and growing difference between the amount the US imported from China and what China imported from America was evidence of trade distorting restrictions that cost US jobs and global market share.

Even if the size of this trade deficit primarily reflects American consumer behaviour, it is true that there are many barriers to US companies operating in China.

China's markets remain opaque; state-owned enterprises continue to dominate key sectors; they and their private sector counterparts receive subsidies and loans at preferential rates, and approval of foreign investment often requires the forced transfer of IP. Despite this, between 2010 and 2020, US companies invested £150 billion in China, principally in the information and technology, automotive, energy and retail sectors – nearly two-thirds of it in greenfield investment rather than acquisitions, in the hope of penetrating the massive Chinese market. US firms also invested a further $60 billion in Chinese start-ups.[21] Berkshire Hathaway's investment in Chinese electric vehicle (EV) manufacturer BYD has been among its most successful in recent years.

The Biden administration shared the same concerns as its predecessor about distortions in the Chinese market, but it has placed a greater focus on the ways in which China is using its newfound economic heft for geopolitical advantage. At the most basic level, China's steady economic growth provides fuel for its growing defence budget, which, while staying at roughly 1.7 per cent of GDP for the past two decades, has risen tenfold from $33 billion in 2003 to $293 billion in 2022, making it by far the second largest after the US.[22]

China is using its growing military clout to change the geopolitical balance of power in the Pacific region, which the US considers, like China, to be vital to its security and prosperity. Starting in 2013, China seized and then built military installations on several reefs and small islands in the South China Sea, most of which are claimed by neighbouring countries. Beijing has ignored the 2016 ruling by the Permanent Court of Arbitration in the Hague that China's occupation of these islands is illegal. China is also using its naval and air forces to challenge Japan and South Korea's control over islands in the East China Sea, ceaselessly sending sorties of fighter aircraft into their airspace, and coastguard and civilian fishing vessels into their maritime zones.

Crucially, China's growing national wealth has helped fund a massive increase in the types and volume of Chinese missiles capable of hitting Taiwan, with over a thousand currently in this category, including some hyper-sonic missiles capable of hitting the island within six to eight minutes.[23] This complicates US contingency planning to deter or prevent an all-out Chinese attack, should Beijing decide this was the only way to force its unification with the mainland.

China has also used its growing economic war chest to back Chinese companies' investments in strategically important countries around the world, from Africa to Latin America. Although these investments sometimes deliver much-needed infrastructure, they do so at high interest rates that then often trap recipients in a spiral of debt, from which they can escape only by handing the assets over to China, as Sri Lanka was forced to do with its port in Hambantota, giving the Chinese state-owned company involved a 99-year lease starting in September 2018. What is described by some Western commentators as Chinese 'debt diplomacy' is rarely planned strategically but, even so, China has been comfortable to lend money to corrupt leaders around the world. As in the case of the government of Najib Razak in Malaysia in 2016, they often benefit personally from the investments and then support China politically on its international agenda.[24]

The near unanimous conclusion among US security analysts and both Republican and Democrat policymakers is that, rather than becoming a 'responsible stakeholder', China is using its newfound economic strength to advance its geopolitical interests in ways that are inimical to those of the US.[25]

The opening salvoes of a new geo-economic Cold War

The US may have woken up to the risks of a more powerful and single-minded China, but what to do? US policymakers can't change the worldview of the Chinese leadership. Instead, along with allies, they are focused on limiting the transfer of security related technologies, protecting themselves from Chinese coercion and providing incentives and disincentives to its future behaviour. In this contest, some of the most important tools at each side's disposal are economic, which puts global economic competition at the centre of the New Cold War in a way that it was not during the last.

Above all, the Trump and Biden administrations zeroed in on the fact that China is not yet capable of producing the most advanced semiconductors that are essential for its high-tech industries and new defence capabilities, especially if they want to incorporate AI tools into their operations. Their design continues to be concentrated in the US and Europe, and their manufacture with their Pacific allies, above all Taiwan and South Korea. The Trump administration took a series of legislative steps to stop US companies from exporting advanced semiconductor technologies to China. It also banned US imports of Chinese telecommunications technologies that they believed could enable Chinese espionage. The Biden administration has kept these restrictions, under the banner initially of 'decoupling' the most sensitive areas of US technology from China. It also expanded them by preventing US companies from selling to China advanced methods of manufacturing their own semiconductors.[26] And in August 2023, it passed an executive order designed to prevent US companies from investing in Chinese production of AI, semiconductors or quantum computing.

China's leaders decry these steps as hostile acts to contain and 'suppress' it. They have retaliated so far by banning Chinese state institutions from using US company Micron's chips in their IT systems; by introducing an informal ban on Chinese state employees using Apple iPhones; and by imposing restrictions on the export of gallium and germanium, two rare earth minerals whose production China dominates and that are essential not only in semiconductor manufacturing, but also in many advanced US defence components.

The CCP, however, started its own journey to reduce China's dependence on imports of critical technology in 2015, when President Xi and then Premier Li Keqiang announced the 'Made in China 2025' programme. This was designed to favour and upgrade China's domestic research, development, innovation and industrial capacity in several advanced sectors, such as semiconductors, robotics, AI and nanotechnologies. After US and other policymakers criticized the programme as protectionist, the CCP introduced in 2020 a more benign sounding policy to promote what it called 'dual circulation' – advocating greater economic self-sufficiency through higher quality domestic growth and less reliance on low-end exports, which, to all intents and purposes, has the same objective.[27]

China has taken other steps to hedge against a deterioration in relations with the US. Since 2016, the government has kept its dollar investments in US Treasuries and related assets steady at roughly $1.9 trillion and cycled its continuing trade surpluses via state-owned banks into global infrastructure projects and global equities.[28] This process accelerated following Putin's full-scale invasion of Ukraine and the Biden administration's unprecedented decision to freeze the Russian Central Bank's dollar reserves in response. And, although China appears uninterested for now in allowing the RMB to compete with the US dollar as an alternative reserve currency, it is encouraging more countries to use its currency to settle the bills for their trade with China. In March 2023, the RMB surpassed the dollar for the first time as the main currency used to settle China's external trade.[29]

The close economic relationship that grew between the US and China after the end of the last Cold War now clashes with a deepening sense of bilateral strategic competition. For the first time in its post-war history, America faces in China a true global competitor; one that could undermine its global influence and accentuate its domestic weaknesses. Handling this complicated relationship requires a long-term, disciplined approach from both sides. The CCP might accept competitive co-existence with the US, provided it can retain strong internal political control and is not prevented from increasing its global influence. But the equally important question is whether the US can bring a consistent approach to how it handles China and designs its policies to manage the New Cold War.

3

America is not all it was

We might expect China to present a shared external challenge around which US policymakers can coalesce, as the Soviet threat did during the last Cold War. Indeed, President Biden used the idea of 'winning the twenty-first century' against China as one of the reasons for his administration's signature spending programmes in 2021–22 on infrastructure, on the green transition and on rebuilding semiconductor production capacity within the country.[1] But raising the spectre of a rising China did nothing to lure Republicans to vote in favour of these bills. Notwithstanding bipartisan consensus that China is the biggest threat to America's future security, it looks unlikely that the New Cold War with China will serve as a unifying political force and help overcome the deep partisan divide troubling the United States.

There is little new about toxic politics in Washington or across the United States. Think of the circumstances leading up to Richard Nixon's resignation after the Watergate scandal; or the battle over the election count in the state of Florida in December 2000, when the US Supreme Court Justices ruled five to four, along party lines, to deny Al Gore's challenge and thereby give the presidency to George W. Bush. But what makes this moment so much more dangerous is that America's internal political battles are undermining its global role as the pole around which other democracies can confidently gather. If the US enters the New Cold War politically fractured and grappling with a sense of growing internal insecurity, this will embolden its adversaries and weaken its allies.

Could America's recent global leadership be a one-off?

Even though it is young, the United States, like every country, carries scars from past wounds into its present. Its history of slavery, the Civil War which was meant to resolve the issue, and the subsequent battles for racial equality continue to stir American domestic political discourse and sharpen regional and social divisions. The weight of history also affects how Americans think about their relations with the rest of the world. Most carry within them an innate sense of national exceptionalism, rooted partly in their geography, which separates them from the continents of Asia and Europe, but also in the choice that either their ancestors or they themselves all made, bar Native Americans, to leave their countries of birth for the more open frontiers and possibilities offered by the United States.

George Washington famously warned his compatriots to 'beware foreign entanglements', lest they be polluted by the geopolitical machinations of the old Europe they had left behind in the seventeenth and eighteenth centuries. During the early nineteenth century, as America watched the great European powers carve up much of the rest of the world into their ocean-spanning empires, then Secretary of State John Quincy Adams drafted what became known as the Monroe Doctrine, named after his President James Monroe. It asserted that intervention in the Americas by European colonial powers would be regarded as a hostile act.

It was hardly surprising therefore that, after eventually joining the UK and France in April 1917 to help defeat imperial Germany in the First World War, the US Congress rejected President Wilson's idea that the US should join the League of Nations. Without America's participation, it was powerless to prevent the return of major war in Europe and Asia. Reflecting popular support for isolationism after the Great Depression, the US Congress also passed a series of Neutrality Acts between 1935 and 1939 to prevent America's potential involvement in a future war that might be sparked by the rise of fascism in Germany and Italy.

It took the shock of Japan's unprovoked attack on Pearl Harbor in 1941 to give President Franklin Roosevelt the political authority to declare war. And it took the experience of being drawn late into two world wars to realize that, if America did not overcome its traditional caution and engage internationally from the outset, then it might be drawn into another global conflict in the future with untold costs to American lives and capital.

After 1945, America's newfound internationalism focused on leading the reconstruction of a devastated Europe and Japan and preventing the spread of communism, whose totalitarian and authoritarian ethos was and is the antithesis of Americans' self-identity.[2] If the Soviet Union were successful in spreading its communist influence, then it could leave America alone and vulnerable, starved not only of friends but also of access to vital trading markets. From this calculus emerged the political consensus for the US to break from its traditional caution and commit itself and its forces to defend its allies in Europe and Asia.

From the perspective of its allies, America was a largely benign if still self-interested and exceptionalist leader, as the British and French discovered in 1956 when the US opposed their intervention against Egypt's President

Gamal Abdel Nasser over control of the Suez Canal; and as all America's allies experienced when the Nixon administration unilaterally pulled the US out of the Gold Standard in 1971, ending America's commitment to exchange other countries' holdings of US dollars for gold at a fixed price. But, throughout the Cold War, even after the Soviet Union lost its momentum in the 1970s and slipped into the quagmire of Afghanistan in 1979, the US continued, at great cost, to extend its protective security umbrella over former foes and allies alike, enabling Germany and Japan to become two of the most successful economies in the world. The collapse of the Soviet Union in 1990 and the retreat of communism from much of the world thereafter cemented America's position as the world's only superpower.

Much of America's willingness to lead, and to pay the costs of leadership, was predicated on the belief that it was upholding a world from which America gained as much as others. Opening its markets to its allies, as it did after the Second World War, made its allies wealthier, which then led them to buy more US products and generate greater returns for US investments in their countries. By the 1980s, the fully recovered European countries were awash with Ford and General Motors cars, Coke and Pepsi, and RCA televisions. When it seemed as if the US might lose some of its economic advantages, it championed major multilateral trade agreements that reduced barriers to trade. And it wasn't shy in leveraging its position as the ultimate guarantor of its allies' security to prise open protected sectors of their economies, as the leaders of a burgeoning Japan experienced in their trade negotiations with Washington in the 1980s.

On balance, the four decades of the first Cold War saw the US mix global leadership with a constant rise in the country's net wealth. But, having plateaued in the 1980s, rates of growth in income for the majority of US citizens tapered off from 1990. America's moment of ultimate geopolitical success coincided with rising inequality between those doing well and those falling behind. The US enters the New Cold War with China, therefore, in a very different mindset. The question for its allies and the rest of the world is whether America will end up retreating into a more isolationist shell or whether it has the political will to sustain its position as the principal defender of the world's liberal democracies in the twenty-first century.

Americans don't think they're winning

The vocal frustration about the costs of being the world's global leader that one hears in the US today has arisen largely because many Americans no longer believe they are winning economically.[3] Most US policymakers have concluded that championing an open domestic economy and providing global leadership to remove the many continuing barriers to international trade is a vote-loser, given that it does not automatically lead to a more prosperous America, as it did from the 1950s through the 1980s.

The collapse of the Soviet Union in 1991 was heralded as a victory for the West over command-led economics. Unsurprisingly, it ushered in a period of deepening economic globalization, largely led by successive US administrations. In 1994, President Clinton signed into law the North America Free Trade Agreement with Canada and Mexico, leading to large-scale US manufacturing investment into the cheaper but proximate labour market south of the border. China's entry into the WTO in 2001 was engineered by the Clinton administration and finalized by the Republican administration of George W. Bush. This greatly reduced most barriers to Chinese exports, and the flood of foreign investment and technology that went into China helped fuel the inflow of ubiquitous, cheaply produced Chinese manufacturing imports into the US.

After thirty or so years of globalization, however, the United States is divided into a country of winners and losers. Winners have prospered in global value-adding services like finance, law, consulting, marketing and design, and in high-technology sectors such as pharmaceuticals, aerospace and digital products and services, all of which tap into world markets and exploit US strengths in intellectual property. Losers are clustered in local services like hospitality and retail and in lower-value manufacturing sectors where a combination of automation and competition from cheaper, foreign labour hollowed out local industries and jobs. By 2015, only some 50 per cent of American thirty-year-olds were earning more than their parents in real terms.[4] The country's overall GDP may have continued to grow, but the rewards flowed mainly to those already at or near the top of the income ladder. Between 2001 and 2016, upper-income families added 33 per cent to their net wealth, whereas middle-income families saw their median net worth fall by 20 per cent and lower-income families by 45 per cent.[5]

As large numbers of both Democrat and Republican voters found themselves on the losing side of globalization, they lost faith in the centrist wings of their parties which had championed its benefits for so long, driving members of Congress away from the centre ground.[6] The emergence of the Tea Party movement in 2009 was the early harbinger of a more insular and socially conservative mood on the fringes of the Republican Party. In 2016, Republican primary voters rejected experienced candidates for the presidency and instead became mesmerized by the mercurial tycoon Donald Trump and his anti-globalist vision to put 'America First'. Similarly, in the Democratic presidential primaries, many Democrats rejected Hillary Clinton, the party leadership's preferred and centrist nominee, and turned to Senators Bernie Sanders and Elizabeth Warren, who railed against liberal economic orthodoxy and argued for a different vision of America's future.

The shocking defeat of Hillary Clinton and Trump's election as the 45th US president in November 2016 had many causes. But it was, in part, a manifestation of widespread popular insecurity about America's position in the global economy. In his inauguration speech on 20 January 2017, Trump angrily decried 'the rusted-out factories, scattered like tombstones across the landscape of our nation', addressing himself squarely to the millions of Americans who had seen their standards of living fall as other countries used open trade and investment to catch up with US manufacturing and technology.

The contrast with China's own exceptional economic rise under globalization, and the role previous administrations had played in this outcome, provided Trump with the perfect anti-establishment narrative. He struck a deep chord when he stated that his predecessors – and American 'big business' – had allowed China to take advantage unfairly of a naive US obsession with the power of open markets, building up its economy at the expense of many American workers. And he was right, in the sense that American exporters did not operate on a level playing field in China.

Trump's legacy

The problem with Trump is that he is wrong even when he is right. He did not use the power of his presidency and the temporary respite of Lighthizer's tariffs to undertake the hard grind of passing laws to raise American competitiveness and productivity, whether through increased investment in education or infrastructure. Instead, he wallowed in his obsessive resentment of the way China and others were 'taking advantage' of America. His first step was to use a national security law to impose tariffs unilaterally on exports of steel and aluminium into the US not just from China, but also from America's European and Pacific allies. These measures gave US steel and aluminium companies a shot in the arm but at the expense of those many other US companies that imported these products to use in their own manufactures. Predictably, Trump's trade policy made no positive difference to the US trade deficit in goods, which grew from $750 billion to $915 billion during his term in office.[7]

But Trump's scepticism about globalization and his approach to trade was not a one-off aberration. Following Joe Biden's tight presidential victory in November 2020, his administration adapted, rather than rejected Trump's economic doctrine. His National Security Advisor, Jake Sullivan, described their approach as a new 'foreign policy for the middle class', meaning the state would focus its policy tools on supporting the creation of American jobs at home, rather than hope that a renewed US commitment to building more open global markets would lead to a positive 'trickle down' into the domestic economy.[8]

The Biden administration rejected the idea of launching or engaging in any new rounds of multilateral or bilateral trade negotiations, whether with allies or other partners, as many of its allies had hoped it would, and as its predecessors had done as part of American leadership during the first Cold War. It maintained the Trump tariffs on Chinese imports and on steel and aluminium imports, including those from America's allies, converting them only into tariff quotas, meaning the tariffs kick back in if imports exceed a particular threshold in a given time period. Biden did not lift the Trump administration's block on the appointment of new appellate judges to the World Trade Organization, undermining the WTO's ability to adjudicate trade disputes, lest some of these judgements go against the US. And the Biden administration's signature

2022 Inflation Reduction Act offered $390 billion over ten years in green energy subsidies and tax credits for new electric vehicle purchases, but only providing these are 'made in America'.

Looking from the outside, the US seems to have shifted from America First under Trump to Americans First under Biden. And there is little let-up on the horizon. Whether Donald Trump becomes the Republican candidate again in the 2024 presidential election or not, his outlook animates the Republican Party base and, therefore, his Republican challengers. Resentment permeates their discourse. Rather than courting internationally minded US businesses, as past Republican candidates had done, Trump's leading challenger, Florida Governor Ron DeSantis, launched a new front against them in the culture war over what he decries as their 'woke' principles to promote greater diversity and inclusion and to fight climate change.

Democrats can point to the fact that, in terms of raw GDP numbers, their policies are working, including their emphasis on subsidizing domestic investment over international economic engagement. GDP growth and employment have bounced back following the COVID pandemic far faster than in other developed economies.[9] And a new wave of US productivity could be unleashed by America's latest pioneering advances in generative AI. But most qualitative measures paint a far more worrying picture; life expectancy rates have fallen to their lowest level in twenty years; low rates of official unemployment (3.8 per cent in September 2023) disguise the fact that the labour force participation rate is stuck at around 62 per cent, with some 10 million Americans looking for work but not classified as employed; and costs of health and education continue to rise steeply, squeezing net disposable income, while low-saving and high-spending Americans' levels of accumulated wealth are much lower than their peers.[10] America may still have its drivers of future dynamism, but most Americans believe the fruits of its wealth are very unevenly distributed.

America hangs back and China steps into the breach

The US has entered the New Cold War in a mood of self-doubt, division, and a growing sense of economic insecurity. So long as Americans are focused on their own journey of national rejuvenation, Biden Democrats and Trump or DeSantis Republicans will be equally reticent to use trade liberalization as an instrument to gain geopolitical advantage. This matters because America will need to rally its allies to challenge China effectively. But what Americans think of themselves and the internecine battles they wage will influence what others think about America and how confident they are to follow its lead.

On this front, the experience of the Trump administration has left deep scars. Early in his term, Trump refused to endorse NATO's Article V commitment that each member of the alliance will come to the aid of the other, implying it was conditional on Europeans importing more US gas as well as spending more on their defence.[11] His threats did more to reawaken European fears of US abandonment than to drive changes in policy. And Trump's demand that Japan and South Korea quadruple the substantial amounts they already paid the US for stationing troops in their countries looked like a protection racket 'shakedown'. It implied that US troops were there as mercenaries, not for American interests, but for those of the hosting country.

The Biden administration has done a lot to repair the damage, but it has a long way to go. The 'Buy America' provisions contained in its green energy subsidies have created the impression among European and Asian allies that its overriding priority is rebooting America, rather than working with them collectively to take on China's mercantilism.

In the meantime, the Biden administration's lack of a meaningful trade policy has left the field open for China, which has continued to reach out to other countries economically, even as America has turned inwards. In Africa, America's commitments of $70 billion since 2019 to help build modern infrastructure have been dwarfed by China's continuing funding, as well as its stock of recent investments. China's trade with Latin America and the Caribbean exploded from $12 billion in 2000 to $495 billion in 2022, making it the region's largest trading partner ahead of the US.[12] And in Asia, China brought about the Regional Comprehensive Economic Partnership that reduced tariffs on trade between it and twenty other countries across the Asia–Pacific region. In contrast, the Biden administration's June 2022 Indo-Pacific Economic Framework provides a forum to coordinate its members' domestic policies on a host of topics that could facilitate greater trade, such as labour rights, the environment and climate, the digital economy, and competition policy; but it offers no new access to the US market.[13]

America enters the New Cold War trying to project a sense of certainty about its commitment to remain a world leader on security, and an economic power that will be a more attractive alternative than China. But looking at today's American politics, it is doubtful that the political will is going to exist in Washington and across the United States to continue playing this role to the same extent as it has in the past.

And there is little prospect that the rare consensus over the China threat will attenuate the deep political divides running through the US. In the near term at least, both Republicans and Democrats will struggle to overcome their country's loss of socioeconomic cohesion, offering radically different ideas about how to rekindle a belief in the power and possibility of the American Dream that energized the US through much of the last Cold War. One of the risks of continuing partisan warfare is that, instead of coming together, the two political parties will resort to a dangerous, escalatory blame game to show who can be toughest on China. This might be the correct calculus if the priority is to keep or regain control of Congress or the keys to the White House. But to America's allies, this looks like a new version of Americans putting America First, with all the external uncertainties that carries.

China is not the only country that has taken advantage of this moment of internal American division. One leader for whom America's self-doubt has proved a powerful strategic motivator is Russian President Vladimir Putin.

4

Russia's new ambitions

The New Cold War is shaping up to be a three-way affair featuring the same main protagonists as the last, with the United States and its allies on one side, and China and Russia, in place of the Soviet Union, on the other. The main difference this time is that Russia has slipped into China's previous role as the junior member of the authoritarian duo.

Putin's attempt in February 2022 to recreate a greater Russia by conquering Ukraine and converting it into a permanent buffer with NATO in Europe has backfired, with two crucial consequences. Russia now faces a new Iron Curtain with its European neighbours to its west and north, which is forcing it to strengthen its defence along both axes. It also needs to find new points of influence over Europe in the Balkans and Africa.

Russia has also been forced to reorientate its economic ties to its south and east, making it heavily dependent on China for its economic future. Putin had made important strides to strengthen Russia's relations with China prior to 2022. But his invasion of Ukraine has forced China to align openly with Putin. After all, a defeated Putin would leave China at the mercy of a resurgent US and NATO. There is a dawning realization in Washington and allied capitals, therefore, that the New Cold War starts with a reversal of America's pivot to China that began in 1972 under Richard Nixon. The US is now up against not only China, but, once again, China and Russia together.

Russia looks back to the future

Russia in 2024 remains a throwback to another era. Its leaders and, as polling shows, a majority of its population, are trapped mentally between abiding pride in their victory in the 'Great Patriotic War' of 1941–45 and shame at the collapse of the USSR in December 1991.[1] The post-1945 USSR gave them status and global power. Economic opportunities and personal freedoms may have been severely constrained, but they were at the heart of an empire that provided protection, stability and reflected glory. For Russia's leaders there was the satisfaction and material benefits of controlling vast natural and military resources, and the international respect and diplomatic influence from wielding them freely around the world in their contest against America and the West.

And then, suddenly, it was all lost. Russia was reduced in eighteen chaotic months to a rump state – still by far the largest in the world by size of territory, spanning eleven time zones, and with all the outward trappings of its post-war status as a great power, including its nuclear warheads and delivery systems. But, as the former Soviet states became independent, Russia lost sovereignty over swathes of Central Asia and much of the valuable territory that it had acquired in eastern Europe and the Caucasus in the eighteenth century under Putin's great heroes and, some say, current role models, Peter the Great and then Catherine the Great. And without the Warsaw Pact, its western borders were no longer as secure as they were during the post-war period.

Measured by size of GDP, Russia's economy also fell from third largest in the world after the US and Japan in 1990 (the USSR's national output then was half America's size: $2.6 trillion to $5.2 trillion), to only the tenth largest in 2022 (by which time Russia's GDP was a little over $2 trillion, compared to America's $25 trillion and China's $18 trillion). This has left Russia's economy smaller than that of Italy and Canada, despite its much larger population and trove of natural resources.[2]

Vladimir Putin and his acolytes blame their predecessors, above all former leader Mikhail Gorbachev, and the US for its humiliations – not themselves. They are blind or indifferent to their role since 2000 in supervising Russia's continuation as a corrupt and overly militarized country and a badly managed fossil fuel economy. They fixate instead on America's triumphalism at the collapse of the Soviet Union; on its failed efforts to help transplant a free market into Russia's unique political economy in the 1990s, and on the gradual loss of Ukraine. This began with US support for the Orange Revolution in 2005, which denied a stolen victory by Russia's preferred candidate, Viktor Yanukovych, and was completed during the Maidan protests in Kyiv which led to the overthrow of Yanukovych when he was president in 2014.

At the core of their resentment has been US support for NATO's post-Cold War enlargement to include former Warsaw Pact members and the Baltic states. The harshest blow was the George W. Bush administration's ill-timed insistence that the NATO summit in Bucharest in 2008 should promise eventual NATO membership to former Soviet states Ukraine, Georgia and Moldova, without a road map to make it happen.

There is no recognition or understanding that the brutality of Soviet rule in Ukraine in the early Soviet era, and in parts of Central and East European states during the last Cold War, spurred the region's new leaders to want to entrench their newfound sovereignty and democracy in the two institutions with a successful track record of delivering these for their members: NATO and the EU.

The Russian leadership's resentment also blinds them to the way in which their own autocratic and inefficient tendencies sharpen their neighbours' historical concerns. In place of NATO enlargement, Russian leaders cynically called for a more inclusive 'common European security architecture', when it was always clear that this would mean giving the Kremlin a veto over how its closest European neighbours could exercise their political and economic sovereignty and ensure their security. The Kremlin's record speaks for itself. All neighbours that it has been able to cajole or coerce into its own post-Cold War structures, from Belarus, to Armenia, to Kyrgyzstan, have opaque systems of government that are hard-wired to give precedence to Russian economic and security interests and make them subservient to Russia's foreign policy.

At heart, Putin still sees the United States as the yardstick by which to measure Russia's security and geopolitical status. Rather than use the boom in commodity prices during the 2010s and a well-educated population to try to modernize Russia's economy, he remains obsessed with retaining the outward trappings of a great power alongside the US, above all on the military front. Putin's main priority has been modernization of Russia's nuclear and conventional forces to keep itself on a par with America.

Behind a new Iron Curtain of his own making

President Putin's obsession with the threat he believes the US still poses to Russia, his fanatical belief in reconstituting a greater Russia and Ukraine's intrinsic position within it, and his determination to leave a legacy worthy of his more than two decades in power led him to make a catastrophic roll of the dice. But launching a 'special military operation' in February 2022 to decapitate Ukraine's elected government and reabsorb Ukraine into Russia was just the latest in a catalogue of errors.

It is widely believed that pro-Russian Ukrainians were involved in poisoning Viktor Yushchenko, the leading candidate for their 2005 presidential election, hoping this would pave the way for their preferred candidate, Viktor Yanukovych. Yushchenko survived and became president after a rerun of a rigged first round of elections. In 2014, Putin pressured Yanukovych, who had become president in 2010, to reject a planned trade agreement with the EU, in favour of closer economic relations with Russia. The ensuing popular protests led to Yanukovych fleeing to Russia, the exposure of his epic levels of corruption, and Putin's decision to annex Crimea rather than risk seeing it – and the vital Black Sea port of Sevastopol – fall under the control of a hostile government in Kyiv.

In 2022, Putin clearly felt the timing was right to complete the job. The US appeared caught somewhere between a moment of strategic weakness, after the botched withdrawal of its troops from Afghanistan, and geopolitical distractedness, given the complexity of managing the growing China threat. But, yet again, he severely misjudged the political mood in Ukraine and the newly found unity and professionalism of its armed forces, following eight years of fighting Russian-backed separatists in the east. He also severely misjudged the extent of Western resolve to support the rights of their democratic neighbour and to reject the return to power politics and forcible changing of international borders after the slaughter and destruction these forces had unleashed through European history.

The impact of Russia's full-scale invasion of Ukraine has been to unify NATO and enlarge it further to the previously staunchly neutral northern European states Finland and Sweden. EU members and other European countries joined the US in imposing unprecedented sanctions on Russia, including freezing its central bank reserves held in their currencies, cutting off access for Russian banks to the SWIFT inter-bank clearing system, and imposing an embargo on most Russian oil imports and on high-technology exports. Germany has shuttered both Nord Stream pipelines supplying Russian gas to itself and its neighbours and, alongside them, is now importing liquefied natural gas (LNG) as well as piped gas from alternative sources. The EU has promised to accept Ukraine as a member, while NATO created a new Ukraine-NATO Council at its summit in Vilnius in July 2023 to enable close and regular military coordination between the alliance and Kyiv. Russia faces the prospect of living next to what Putin adviser Sergei Karaganov bitterly described to me in 2022 as an 'anti-Russia' Ukraine on its border.

The Russian relationship with its European neighbours is broken. At the time of writing, the war in Ukraine rages on, and some type of conflict is likely to persist at a more or less intense level at least for as long as Putin remains in the Kremlin; after all, he cannot give up the newly annexed Ukrainian territories *and* survive. Nor can the Ukrainian government or its European neighbours let him claim victory or they will open the door to further aggression. Even if there is a ceasefire or armistice, it will be followed by years of litigation about compensation for Russia's well-documented war crimes and negotiation over financial reparations for Ukrainian reconstruction. Under the most optimistic of scenarios, Europeans will never allow themselves to be as dependent on Russia again for their energy security as they were in the 2000s. The proportion of the public and political figures actively sympathetic to Russia in its confrontation with the West (what the Germans call

'Putin *versteher*') has been reduced to a radical minority and, while they are politically disruptive and could be influential again in the future, they cannot turn the clock back to 2021.[3] From Germany to Spain, countries that were historically ambivalent about criticizing Russia have been jolted into a new outlook by Putin's actions and his troops' barbarity. Even Emmanuel Macron now advocates Ukrainian membership of the EU and NATO.[4]

Ukraine could end up somewhat like West Germany through the last Cold War, a heavily armed and partially divided country on the eastern edge of democratic Europe; committed to its reunification and backed in this goal by the US and its allies. Ukraine's eventual membership of NATO and the EU is distant but highly likely. And Russia will be behind a new Iron Curtain, one which is drawn much closer to Russia's western heartland than it was previously.

Putin's policy adjustments add fuel to the fire

Given Putin's actions and the Western responses, today's new stand-off between Russia, Europe and the US carries with it many echoes of the last Cold War. But the balance of forces has changed radically. Putin's Russia does not have the conventional military superiority in Europe that the USSR once had. In March 2014, shortly after Putin's annexation of Crimea, President Obama called Russia 'a regional power' that threatened its neighbours, 'not out of strength but out of weakness'. Obama's demotion of Russia from its global status infuriated Putin.[5]

But Putin, like his predecessors, is resourceful. If Russia cannot keep up with America economically or match it militarily, then it can at least try to undermine it and its allies. Asymmetric warfare, especially misinformation and disinformation, was a tool of the Soviet

Union in the last Cold War. Today, America's internal political travails and the advent of AI-infused social media have given Russia incentive and space to go on the offensive, amplifying the partisan divide within the US, especially over cultural issues. This is one of the domains where Yevgeny Prigozhin, founder of the Wagner Group and until the summer of 2023 and his subsequent violent death one of Putin's most loyal confidants, cut his teeth. His 'Internet Research Agency', a state-funded social media troll farm with hundreds of employees working on everything from creating fake personas to search engine optimization, was indicted by the US Department of Justice in 2018 for its widespread interference in the 2016 US presidential election campaign, which, by Facebook's own account, reached as many as 126 million people. Following Trump's victory, they were even accused of staging one rally to support the president-elect while organizing another to oppose him, 'both in New York, on the same day'.[6]

Russia is also seeking to disrupt America's room for manoeuvre globally. Putin has moved from successfully defending Syrian President Bashar al-Assad and Russia's vital sea and air bases on the Mediterranean shore after the popular uprising in 2013–15 on to the offensive, using his victory in Syria to reinsert Russia into the corridors of power in the Gulf and broader Middle East. The creation of OPEC+ in 2016 allows Saudi Arabia and Russia to coordinate their rates of oil production more closely, increasing Russian leverage over the global economy as well as over the pricing of its most valuable export.

Putin and his cohort of 'private' military companies (all backed by Russian military intelligence) are also taking advantage of America's focus on China and Ukraine to spread their tentacles across Africa, Latin America and other resource-rich parts of the world. Moscow has engineered or endorsed a series of coups across the Sahel region between 2021 and 2023, leveraging chronic Islamist militancy, extreme poverty and weak governments, as well as post-colonial resentment against France and Europe and the Soviet Union's past support for African independence movements. The insertion of troops from the Wagner Group to back these military juntas allows them to siphon funds from the sale of precious metals and other commodities, while propping up the coup leaders using not only Wagner's ruthless mercenaries but also its deft use of information operations.

Increasing Russian influence in the Sahel also provides Putin with an important new front from which to try to destabilize Europe; driving illegal migration northwards, and potentially disrupting the sale of commodities for Europe's green transition or blocking new energy supply lines. Niger – the latest country in the Sahel to fall to a Moscow-backed military coup – is a critical transit route for the gas Nigeria hopes to transfer to Europe, as well as an important source of uranium for Europe's nuclear power.

While Putin may congratulate himself on the adroitness of his tactical adjustments to the growing stalemate in Europe, his actions promise to be as strategically counter-productive in the long term as his full-scale invasion of Ukraine. Rather than fragmenting the US, Putin's actions since 2015 have united the majority of Republicans and Democrats in Congress against him. Many Trump supporters in the Republican Party consider Ukraine a failed state and link President of Ukraine Volodymyr Zelenskyy to what Trump calls 'the Biden crime family'. But there is strong opposition to Putin on both sides of the aisle. It is notable that the US increased its sanctions against Russia and tripled the funding for the Obama-era European Deterrence Initiative during President Trump's term in the White House.[7]

For their part, Europeans are responding to the new Russian threat by deepening their levels of economic integration and political coordination. All European governments are diversifying their sources of gas and oil imports for the long term. Many are building new plants to re-gasify LNG imports and new pipelines to transport the gas to where it is needed at a breakneck pace. EU members have issued collective debt for the first time to accelerate the roll-out of the infrastructure for their transition to renewable power and transportation. They have created new collective mechanisms to acquire ammunition and other military equipment, while raising their defence budgets. The movement of Wagner forces into Belarus after their brief mutiny in June 2023 has increased political support for Poland, despite long-standing concerns over backsliding on the rule of law in the country. And Britain and the EU have come together to support Ukraine, despite their ongoing post-Brexit disputes.

Rather than learn from his past failures and likely future setbacks, Putin and his entourage are past masters at doubling down. His State of the Nation Address in April 2023 made it clear that he intends to use this moment of crisis to mobilize Russian citizens around the idea that their country is at war with NATO. Putin will be more secure if he can focus the country's attention on the need to counter a persistent enemy and use this to cement internal political control, rather than opting for a compromise that might reveal his failure to achieve his original goals. The war in Ukraine has given him the opportunity to take Russia from a captured democracy to a full-scale, unabashed autocracy, in which no criticism is tolerated and where the youth are being methodically inculcated in a nationalist triumphalism and xenophobic hatred of the West.[8]

Whereas China learned techniques of societal control from the Soviets during the last Cold War, now the Russian leadership is learning from the Chinese how to use the tools of modern media and digital surveillance to insulate their population more methodically from the truth. Which brings us to another critical difference between this Cold War and the last: Putin's decision to pivot not only Russia's economic infrastructure but also its foreign policy ambitions away from Europe towards China, and through China to countries in the Global South.

The new Russia–China axis

The perspective of a new, long Cold War in Europe has driven Putin to align Russia more closely with China, despite the self-evident risks that its vast neighbour poses to Russia's long-term economic and physical security. And it is now in China's interest to align with Russia, given America's more determined efforts to confront China's rise.

It is true that the two countries are deeply suspicious of each other, given centuries of contest over their lengthy 4,300-kilometre border, including during most of the last Cold War and especially after Stalin's death which opened the 'Sino-Soviet split'. Since the dissolution of the Soviet Union, Russians fear becoming over-dependent on their neighbour, whose large population, giant cities and itinerant citizens abut vast swathes of empty Russian territory. There is also growing competition over influence in the former Soviet states of Central Asia. But current geopolitics push China and Russia together; they both fear far more the encroachment of the US and its alliances into what they see as their spheres of influence.

Like Russia, China resents the way it is hemmed in by the United States in its own neighbourhood, through America's military presence along the first island chain around China's coast. This stretches from Japan's main islands in the north, through the Japanese Ryukyu Islands (including

Okinawa) and Taiwan in the middle, to the Philippines in China's south. When Beijing criticizes America's 'Cold War mentality' it is drawing attention to the parallels between US support for NATO's post-Cold War expansion in Europe, and the Biden administration's strengthening of its security relations with its allies in the Pacific region.

In the face of what they view as a hostile America, there is a clear logic to Russia and China standing 'back to back', metaphorically and physically. Xi Jinping reinforced the centrality of China's relationship with Russia during his three-day visit to Moscow on 20–22 March 2023. Their joint statement on 4 February 2022 that 'the friendship between the two States has no limits' and that 'there are no "forbidden" areas of cooperation', is taking many forms.

The Chinese and Russian navies and air forces have increased their tempo of joint military exercises, both close to home, for example with joint air patrols of the Taiwan Strait, and globally, in the eastern Mediterranean and, in February 2023, joining with the South African navy for a three-way exercise in the Indian Ocean off the port of Durban.[9] Russia has been the main external defence supplier to China, accounting for 81 per cent of the country's defence imports between 2017 and 2021. Now, Chinese companies are becoming increasingly important for Russia as it desperately seeks to source drones and other dual-use technologies and components, such as semiconductors, for its war in Ukraine. While historically they have been cautious about selling China its most advanced military technology, the Russians may be tempted to exchange higher value defence exports in return.[10]

Economically, China–Russia trade has more than doubled from $107 billion in 2018 to over $220 billion in 2023, its highest ever level.[11] Unlike during the last Cold War, China can engage with Russia confident in the knowledge that it will at least be an equal and that it may soon have the upper hand strategically in their economic relationship. For example, since Europe's sanctions on Russia over Ukraine, imports of Chinese cars have grown sevenfold, raising China's market share from 7 per cent in 2021 to 49 per cent in 2023, rapidly replacing the European brands that had dominated the Russian market since the 1990s. Moscow Mayor Sergei Sobyanin's boast in July 2023 about the revival of the Soviet-era Moskvich car plant glosses over the fact that the cars emerging from the former Renault-owned factory are made using kits and engines purchased from China.[12]

Russia is also now being forced to accelerate a major shift in its gas pipeline network and commodity exports from their traditionally east–west axis to north–south, as it seeks to compensate for the lost European markets by supplying the growing demand in China and Asia. China spent $88 billion on imports of Russian oil, coal, LNG and pipeline gas in the twelve months to February 2023, up from $57 billion in the previous twelve months.[13] Discussions are under way to approve a second pipeline (Power of Siberia 2) that would double the 40 billion cubic metres per annum that is projected to be delivered to China from the recently completed Power of Siberia 1. China is also investing heavily in the new port infrastructure Moscow needs to develop the Northern Sea Route through the rapidly warming Arctic Sea, offering faster and cheaper alternatives to the Suez Canal for delivering Chinese and other trade to Europe.[14]

This Sino-Russian strategic alignment has major geopolitical consequences. But there is an additional dimension to their contest with the US and its allies, that goes beyond pure geopolitics: whose system of political governance and vision of international order will dominate the twenty-first century?

5

The ideological roots of the New Cold War

Political ideology plays a central role in the New Cold War. But the difference this time is that leaders in Beijing and Moscow no longer promote a shared communist ideology. Instead, they are united by a determination to protect their sovereignty from internal and external subversion. They prioritize the rights of the state over the rights of the individual, both at home and in the kind of governments and governance they support around the world.

This helps to spur their contest with the US and its allies because each side sees the other's system not only as flawed but also as a threat. The Chinese and Russian leaderships believe that democratic systems of government undermine state power. America's gridlocked politics and the assault on the US Capitol on 6 January 2021 have confirmed their view, as did the US and Europe's devastating failures to impose democracy in Afghanistan, Iraq and Libya. For their part, democratic leaders believe that autocratic governments led by strongmen contain the seeds of their own collapse and tend to engage in external adventurism as a means of stemming the inevitable. Putin's war on Ukraine is the latest example.

The competition between these two systems of government has spread to the UN, which the old Soviet Union and US used principally as a theatrical backdrop for their competition. This time, China is making a sustained effort to shift the norms underpinning UN institutions to favour the rights of its member governments over the rights of the individuals that the UN system is meant to protect. This has sharpened European concerns over China's growing global power.

My system is best

Despite stating its partnership with Russia has 'no limits', China has been careful not to provide Russia with material support for its war against Ukraine, whether by supplying it with weapons or helping the Kremlin to evade financial sanctions. It has thereby avoided stepping over the red lines the Biden administration drew for imposing sanctions on countries or entities supporting Russia's war effort.

But its leadership's refusal to condemn the invasion and parroting of the Russian narrative that it was provoked by NATO, along with conspiracy theories about the existence of US biological weapons laboratories in Ukraine, reveals a deeper truth that is severely damaging for US and allied perceptions of China. Even if the conflict in Ukraine comes to a halt, and even if China plays some role in this outcome, the close alignment between Beijing and Moscow will persist in other ways that will feed and sustain the New Cold War. Why? Because China and Russia's partnership is not just about geopolitics – it is about ideology.

Chinese and Russian leaders no longer espouse a shared Marxist–Leninist worldview, as they once did. Nationalism, fed by resentment of past humiliations, and revanchism, driven by the determination to right historical wrongs, are now much more potent connectors. Above all, their countries' histories have convinced them of the indispensability of having a strong state to protect their sovereignty from external intervention. And a strong state is not viable if its leadership is under constant siege from internal political competition. For leaders in both Beijing and Moscow, the separation of powers between the executive, legislative and legal branches of government that lies at the root of 'liberal' democratic systems of governance, and the existence of a vibrant and independent civil society and media, are sources of domestic insecurity. To them, the British referendum vote in favour of leaving the EU in 2016, the endless internal negotiations within the EU on economic and foreign policy, and the 6 January 2021 insurrection in Washington DC rejecting the results of the US presidential election all confirm democracy's inherent dysfunctionality. Plus, the abject failure and chaos that has followed Western efforts to introduce institutions of democratic governance into post-conflict societies since 2000 makes Beijing and Moscow even more determined to prevent the spread of democracy into their countries and regions.

Both countries are led instead by single parties – the CCP and United Russia – which represent and address the interests of the state. United Russia nominally stands for elections against a group of opposition parties, but this is a charade in which their potential routes to power are perennially blocked. True political opposition is banned. Law courts act under instruction from the government. And, since the invasion of Ukraine, Russian media has become almost as tightly controlled as China's.

The other commonality is that the party leadership in both countries is now organized around a single domineering leader who sits at the top of all decision-making. Putin led the way. He has served as president of Russia since 2000, with just a brief four-year stint as prime minister after his first eight as president. He returned to the Kremlin in

2012, and then, with all organs of power under his control, passed a constitutional amendment that would start the clock on two new six-year terms as president after the next elections in 2024. With no meaningful party structure to check Putin's vision, he could potentially remain in power until 2036.

However, the shift from one-party to one-man rule has been most notable in China.[1] After the chaos of the Cultural Revolution, the CCP decided to avoid the risks of a return to a single 'great helmsman' and introduced instead a more collective approach to its party leadership. General secretaries of the party, who also serve as presidents of the government and heads of state of the country, were restricted by convention to two five-year terms, in line with the term limits imposed since 1982 on the presidency. The leader made their likely successor a member of the Standing Committee of the Politburo at the start of their second term. Although there are no democratic elections in China, these handovers, from Deng Xiaoping to Jiang Zemin to Hu Jintao to Xi, created a form of check on the leader's supreme power and encouraged intra-party competition between alternative visions about how to manage the country's future.

In March 2018, at the formal start of Xi's second term, the party did away with term limits on the presidency, opening the way for Xi to serve as president of the country and general secretary of the party indefinitely. There are many potential reasons for this shift, among them the view that the party needed to reassert control over itself and the country after the chaotic boom years of economic opening, with its attendant increase in corruption, and that, with a more geopolitically tense world, the benefits of consistent leadership would outweigh its potential risks. When the CCP revised its constitution at the 19th Party Congress in October 2017 to say that 'Party, government, military, civilian, and academic; *east, west, south, north, and centre, the*

Party leads everything', it was a clear statement that the CCP would brook no challenge.[2]

While it is hard to know the full extent to which Xi has successfully centralized power around himself and his loyal followers, the majority view is that he has. One important sign is that Xi Jinping's canon of writing and speeches on how to achieve his 'China Dream' of national rejuvenation, known as 'Xi Jinping Thought', was elevated in 2020 to the same level as Mao Thought, putting the two on a political par.[3] It has long been said that Chinese citizens are all subject to rule by whatever the CCP decides is the law rather than 'the rule of law'. With Xi now in full control of the party, rule by law means rule by Xi.

This is the antithesis of a liberal democracy, in which the separation of powers, an independent judiciary and a strong civil society provide the foundational protections and the institutional scaffolding for the rule of law. The law is upheld by national courts answering to domestic legislation and informed by international law; they ensure that government protects and does not abuse individual rights. These rights are enshrined in the UN's Universal Declaration of Human Rights and the European Convention on Human Rights, among others, as well as in international constitutions and laws of all democracies. These then protect law-making from illegal executive interference and individuals from state predation. They protect individual and corporate property from state capture, and civil society and media from partisan government interference, thereby fostering transparency and limiting corruption. This system of checks and balances has underpinned the relative economic outperformance by liberal democracies and has protected their relative political stability compared to most autocracies.

China's recent record of economic and political stability does not automatically mean it offers a viable alternative.

It is important to remember that it was the CCP that cast the Chinese people into abject poverty between 1949 and 1980, with up to 20 million people perishing in the famine that followed the Great Leap Forward and hundreds of thousands in the Cultural Revolution. In the thirty-four years since violently putting down the popular protests in Tiananmen Square in 1989, the CCP has succeeded in raising GDP per capita in China from $310 to $12,000 with only occasional societal disturbances. This is an impressive feat, but it is not proof of the superiority or the sustainable efficacy of China's political system.

My system should be the world's

One of the main criticisms of autocratic governments in the modern era is that they contain the seeds of their own decline and eventually engender domestic revolt against the single leader or flame out in violent conflict. The leaders of post-independence Iraq, Syria and Belarus spent more time and money trying to hold on to power than improving the state of their country. Imperial and Nazi Germany, Tsarist Russia and Qing dynasty imperial China all ended in war and chaos. Everything seems to be fine in dictatorships until it isn't or, as one of Ernest Hemingway's characters described going bankrupt in his 1927 novel *The Sun Also Rises*, it happened 'gradually, then suddenly'. It is rare in modern history that an autocrat can hand over power smoothly or bloodlessly, especially to a democracy: General Pinochet in Chile and General Franco in Spain are two of the few examples of the latter.

Given the insecurities that are hard-wired into single-party systems and dictatorships, successful and unsuccessful autocratic leaders spend a large amount of their time and their country's resources ensuring there are no internal threats to their power. China's budget for internal security is estimated to be about 7 per cent larger than its defence budget.[4] But internal insurrection is often abetted from the outside, which means they also spend a lot of time trying to prevent the rise of external threats to their domestic power.

Today, China and Russia are focused on building a more permissive international environment for their political system. Xi Jinping and Vladimir Putin frequently claim they want to build a more 'democratic', multipolar world; in other words, one that has more voices at the table and that is not US-led or US-dominated.[5] But this disguises the fact that they are entirely uninterested in whether the additional governments seated at decision-making tables represent the will or interests of their citizens. What both leaders want is a world that is safer for autocratic forms of governance.

Their priority is to gather around them as many govern-ments as possible whose approach to domestic governance and international order matches their own. Hence, China's unhesitating financial and political support for dictators around the world, from Venezuela to Zimbabwe, irrespect-ive of their abuses of their citizens' human rights or their failure to deliver progress for their countries – even, it seems, of their ability to repay their debts to Beijing. This is because the most important message that China and Russia want to communicate is that they reject 'interference in the internal affairs' of other countries, because national sovereignty is supreme.

And yet, hypocritically, they do interfere in other coun-tries' internal affairs, providing it is to stem the spread of democracy. China readily backed the military junta in Myanmar after its brutal 2020 coup against an elected parliament; it props up the murderous Kim Jong Un and his regime in North Korea. China and Russia provide material support to the Iranian regime as it executes its way out of the latest popular protests against its failed policies. Having helplessly witnessed the 'colour revolutions' of the 2000s in Ukraine, Georgia and Armenia, and then successfully blocked one in Syria, Russia has also pivoted to a more activist strategy. The Kremlin is helping small groups take power in strategically important African countries the old-fashioned way: through a coup, followed by the provision of mercenaries to help keep the coup leaders in power.

Further betraying their self-serving interpretation of more democratic international relations, both countries support the idea of spheres of influence, whereby the biggest countries gain privileges in their neighbourhood by dint of their size and power. Putin supports those neighbouring leaders who swear fealty to him and prevent the entry of democratic politics, regardless of the negative impact on the countries concerned, such as Ukraine under Yanukovych and Belarus under Lukashenko. Or he backs separatist movements inside nations whose loyalty he doubts, such as in Transnistria in Moldova and South Ossetia and Abkhazia in Georgia. China believes territorial disputes in the South China Sea should be resolved bilaterally – in other words through negotiations where it holds the upper hand.

Beijing and Moscow's shared views of how to preserve international order are diametrically opposed to the democratic approach, which holds that democratic governance, for all its flaws, is the only system under which countries and their societies can flourish sustainably in the long term. One of the key lessons in Europe from the rise of Nazism and totalitarianism ahead of the Second World War is that democratic governance is not only good for the nation, society and the individual, it also lessens the risk of war. This is because autocratic leaders generally end up externalizing their internal insecurity. Putin needs buffer countries in central and eastern Europe not because he believes that NATO will attack Russia, but because he wants to keep the example of successful democratic governments, which pose a threat to the survival of his regime, as far from Russia as possible. The more he worries about his hold on power, the more he is tempted to try to reinforce his position domestically by changing the status quo externally, as he did by launching his full-scale invasion of Ukraine.

For his part, Xi Jinping has stated that Taiwan must reunify with mainland China by 2049. But it is fair to question whether he or his successors can wait that long. The CCP views Taiwan as the last piece of the puzzle that would reconstitute greater China after it was dismembered during the century of humiliation. It is not just that its 'return to China' would bring glory to the CCP, Taiwan also represents the missile of democracy aimed at the legitimacy of China's one-party communist system. If Xi felt he was losing his grip on the economy or party politics at some point in the coming years, he might decide he has to accelerate reunification by all means possible so as to shore up his and the party's position at home.

The battle for universal values

The collapse of the Soviet Union and the supremacy of the United States at the end of the last Cold War gave a new impetus to liberal democracy as the ideal system of domestic governance for countries across the world. By 2000, there were 120 democracies, 63 per cent of the total number of countries recognized by the UN, and the highest number ever recorded.[6]

There was little reason to believe that it would stop there. But the rise of China with its alternative political model coincided with a series of failures by democratic governments to deliver on their promise of prosperity and stability. The Global Financial Crisis in the US and Europe in 2008–12 severely tarnished US-style, free market economics and led to the rise of more defensive populist politics. In Latin America, Argentina's economic instability reignited Peronist populism, and Venezuela's democracy was taken hostage by Hugo Chávez and his successor Nicolás Maduro. And the successful model offered by Chile's centrist governments collapsed into partisan gridlock and social violence in 2019. In Africa, the recent coups in the Sahel come on the heels of a series of economic failures, such as in Ghana and Zambia.[7] In South Africa, the African National Congress, which has been elected six times consecutively to govern the country since the end of apartheid, has led it into deepening economic malaise and corruption.

All of which leads the Chinese to ask: why do you believe your system of government is superior to ours? Is the Western emphasis on protecting the political rights of individuals universally correct or does it reflect the privileged perspective of the wealthy? The CCP prides itself on pursuing what can be translated as 'the mass line'; the idea that the business of good government is to give the most people the best outcome possible. From their perspective, this starts with economic rights.[8]

While no elected leader would deny the centrality of delivering prosperity to their citizens, democratic systems emanate from the idea of individual choice. A government is chosen by the people to serve them. People do not serve the government to help deliver its idea of what is best for them. Hence the right to vote; to protest; to take the government to court; to prevent unnecessary official intrusion into privacy and personal data. And because all individuals matter, democracies also place emphasis on protecting the rights of minorities and promoting the interests of the underprivileged. Democracy is not the tyranny of the majority.

Democracies have made enormous strides in the past fifty years to give women an equal voice in political decision-making. Contrast this with the patriarchal approach in China, where there are no women on the twenty-four-member Politburo of the CCP, after the one woman on it was not replaced at the Party Congress in October 2022, and there are only eleven women on the party's 205-member Central Committee.[9] The CCP is as determined to suppress local groups promoting women's rights as it is environmental NGOs and labour unions – lest they challenge the CCP's monopoly on political power.

Authoritarian governments such as those in China and Russia tend to favour a cultural conservatism that endorses patriarchal power and thinking. In Russia, which now recognizes the special role of the Russian Orthodox Church, church and state are united in the service of each other, not leading their separate domains as they do in democracies. Patriarch Kirill, leader of the Church, is one of the most vocal supporters of Putin's war in Ukraine. The Church has received large financial injections from the state over the past twenty years to rebuild its presence at home, to support allied orthodox patriarchates abroad and, it seems, for the Patriarch himself, if the photo of him wearing a $30,000 Breguet watch in 2009 is to be taken at face value.[10]

But China's relative success to date in delivering economic growth and modernization and improved living standards to its people makes the authoritarian model more attractive to many than the democratic alternative. Since 2005, the world has entered what the respected NGO Freedom House has described as a 'democratic recession', cutting the number of fully democratic countries back to 84 out of 195.[11] Decisive autocrats like Mohammed bin Salman in Saudi Arabia, Paul Kagame in Rwanda or Nguyễn Phú Trọng of Vietnam lead countries that are on the rise. And the elected leaders of rising democracies – Modi in India, or Erdoğan in Turkey – flirt with autocracy by undercutting the checks and balances in their political systems that enabled them to be elected in the first place.

This shift in the ideological balance of power is most visible in the battle at the United Nations for the values that guide the UN system. China has embarked on a multi-year, sustained campaign to challenge the values underpinning the UN's Universal Declaration of Human Rights, which place individual rights, democracy and the rule of law as the foundational principles of good governance and, critically, international peace. The UN's Human Rights Council provides a good window into this contest. The Council is responsible for ensuring UN members respect freedom of association and assembly, freedom of expression, freedom of belief and religion, women's rights, LGBT rights and the rights of racial and ethnic minorities. And yet its elected members to terms spanning 2021–25 include Algeria, China, Cuba, Kazakhstan, Kyrgyzstan, Qatar, the UAE, Vietnam and, until it was suspended in 2022, Russia, whose governments either barely tolerate or actively reject these principles.

One area where the clash of values is intensifying is over global governance of the internet. Having invested vast resources into building its own digital ecosystem behind the 'Great Firewall', Chinese companies are now helping developing economies around the world build their own digital infrastructures, under the banner of the 'Digital Silk Road'. Alongside the capacity to roll out smart transportation systems and online government services comes the opportunity to install Chinese-style surveillance systems of their citizens. This is a very attractive proposition to governments around the world that share a similar approach to China's on political governance. And it provides China with a growing group of states willing to back its agenda for reforming the rules of the road for global internet governance.

To the extent that the US and its allies resist these changes, the world is likely to witness a gradual splintering of the internet into distinct, less interoperable digital domains, each governed according to their own political principles. This will cement geopolitical divisions and provide more fuel for the New Cold War.

The aligned efforts of China and Russia to draw others to their side in ways that undermine the democratic values of the post-war era are driving European governments into a more proactive posture alongside the United States in the sharpening geopolitical contest. Not only are they standing up to Putin in Ukraine, but they are also lining up more explicitly with the US in its global competition with China, despite some deep misgivings about the practicality and predictability of US policies. They are determined not to concede the hard-won democratic gains of the twentieth century in the twenty-first.

6

A renewed transatlantic partnership

Whereas Europe was the epicentre of the last Cold War, now it is part of a more complex and multi-faceted geo-political geometry. Following Vladimir Putin's brazen invasions of Ukraine, Russia is once again the main threat to European security. But the United States, Europe's indispensable ally and protector against a revanchist Russia, is focused on building a common front against China, which is in many ways a more distant challenge and, currently, Europe's principal economic trading partner.

Europeans understand they need to cooperate with the US to counter Chinese and Russian efforts to project their authoritarian values globally. They have also been jolted out of their sanguine attitude to deepening economic interconnections with China by the shocking way that Russia weaponized Europe's energy dependence over Ukraine. But Europeans fear the economic costs of taking on Russia and China simultaneously. They are also concerned that America's China policy – especially towards Taiwan – could be compromised by internal US partisan competition. The risk is that their ambivalence towards the threats posed by China could lead Washington to reduce its commitment to Europe, just as they depend once again on the US for their security.

As a result, European governments are taking the US side in the New Cold War, issuing new policies to reduce their economic and technological dependence on China, and Indo-Pacific strategies to help the US counterbalance China's growing influence in the region. China's hopes that Europe would find an 'independent' middle way between it and the US are quickly receding. Instead, China's alignment with Russia over the war in Ukraine means that Europeans are preparing for a new, two-front Cold War – in Europe and in the Indo-Pacific.

Europe between America and China

Long before Putin's invasion of Ukraine, Americans made the point forcefully to their European allies that the biggest threat to a liberal democratic conception of international order came from China.[1] As the principal custodians of peace and security in the Asia–Pacific, through whose sea lanes passes much of the trade on which the US and its European and Asian allies depend, American policymakers have long believed that they should set the terms of Western policy towards China, and that Europe should be loyal followers. Whenever they have hesitated, as over plans in 2005 to lift the 1989 EU arms embargo on China or, more recently, to use cheap Huawei kit to deliver a rapid European roll-out of 5G communications infrastructure, Europeans have come under severe US pressure to change course. After a fraught six months in 2005, the EU arms embargo remains in place nearly twenty years later. And several European countries, including the UK, have been forced to evict Huawei from their 5G networks after the Trump administration placed it and other Chinese telecommunications companies on the US 'Entity List', banning their use of US semiconductor technologies and designs without express US authorization.

US insistence on leading the way in the transatlantic approach to China has caused some resentment and frequent resistance by European governments and businesses and EU institutions. Of the several reasons for this resistance, the most obvious is economic. Europe depends more on exports to drive economic growth than the United States, with its more dynamic and diverse domestic economy. After opening up in the 1980s, China became a principal destination for European exports, above all those from Germany, which had precisely the right mix of products and technologies to help China develop a modern economy. Its machine tools and chemicals helped China establish the basic manufacturing base for its own early exports. Further, Germany's reliable, well-designed cars and French and Italian luxury brands fed its growing consumer market. As Germany's exports to China expanded, likewise did Germany's demand for inputs from its central European neighbours, raising the economic tide for the EU as a whole. From 2010, China deepened its economic relationship with Europe by recycling part of its growing trade surplus into inward investment into European companies and infrastructure.[2] Lacking the same deep pools of private capital as the US, these investments were very welcome in Europe.

Restricting trade with China at the same time as with Russia is a far more costly proposition in European capitals than it is in Washington. Having already taken a big hit to their economic competitiveness by shutting off most cheap Russian energy, cutting back on their exports to China at the same time would be hard to swallow. In contrast, Washington stands to make some gains. European countries imported 141 per cent more LNG from the US in 2022 compared to 2021, making it Europe's top supplier and accounting for 64 per cent of total US LNG exports, as they sought to replace Russian supplies.[3] Europeans already buy about half their defence equipment from the US, meaning American arms producers can expect a further boost as European defence budgets surged by 13 per cent in 2022 to $345 billion to build an effective deterrent against Putin.[4] At the same time, European exporters to the US must compete with American companies that now benefit from access to far cheaper domestic energy production and the Biden administration's large subsidies for the US transition to green energy.

While many in Europe are warning about the risks of deepening economic relations that fuel China's authoritarian rise, it is a tough sell for European governments to heed this advice. The China threat is distant, whereas Russia's is proximate. Only France and the UK – the former with its Pacific Island territories and the latter with its Five Power Defence Arrangements to provide security assistance to four countries in the region – have any formal security commitments in the Asia–Pacific. And there is no sense in European capitals or among the public that they are in a zero-sum contest to be the top power in the world, militarily or technologically. Europe lost that crown some time ago.[5]

Instead, there is considerable distrust among European leaders about US motivations and policies towards China, above all concerning Taiwan. America's China strategy appears to be spinning into the whirlpool of Washington's polarized and partisan domestic politics. When, on his return from a four-day visit to China in April 2023, President Macron complained to the press that Europe should have an independent Taiwan policy, he was voicing the concerns of many; his mistake was to voice his concerns publicly.[6]

Donald Trump's blunt use of US tariffs against China in 2017, and often bullying tactics to block European use of Chinese technologies, were some of the reasons behind calls for EU members to develop greater 'strategic autonomy' from the US. Many believed that by developing their own China strategy as part of this process, they would have greater agency in the contest with China than they did in the contest with the Soviet Union.[7] They could also keep open avenues for cooperation on meeting global challenges of equal concern to Europe and China, such as combating climate change. Here, China promised to be potentially a more constructive partner than the US, with its large domestic supplies of fossil fuels and climate-sceptic Congress. Aware of European concerns, the Chinese leadership has worked hard to convince European leaders to forge a third way between America's outright hostility and an impossible open embrace.

Europeans have woken up to the extent of the China challenge

The heyday of 'win–win' Europe–China cooperation was relatively short-lived, however. Ever since 2015, the shine has been coming off the relationship. The German phrase *Wandel durch Handel* – transformation through trade – captured the idea that had also animated the Clinton administration in the 1990s: drawing China into economic globalization and interdependence would trigger gradual political opening there. But Xi Jinping's rise to power in 2012 and his heavy-handed reimposition of centralized political control shattered this self-satisfying myth that many European politicians and business leaders had maintained to justify their deepening relationship with China.

Whereas the hardening of US attitudes to China is driven principally by geopolitical competition, the loss of Europe's innocence about its relationship with CCP-led China rests on Beijing's trampling of the democratic human rights and commitments to upholding international law that are central to the EU's political identity and its vision of what constitutes a stable international order.

Europeans watched in dismay as Xi transitioned from the justifiable campaign against corruption in the CCP, People's Liberation Army and state-owned enterprises to the jailing of lawyers representing those charged with challenging the authority of the party. Most damaging was the mass incarceration of some one million members of the Muslim Uighur population in the province of Xinjiang as a way of crushing once and for all an ethnic and religious identity that a small number had used as reason to carry out lethal terrorist attacks in the province and in Beijing. There was no disguising the fact that, rather than leaning towards political liberalization, the CCP had used China's growing wealth to double down on its autocratic system.

The same pattern played out in Hong Kong. However reprehensible some of the attacks were by young pro-democracy activists there on the police, public property and the legislative assembly, the disproportionate use of the all-encompassing National Security Law that Beijing imposed on Hong Kong in June 2020 showed that Xi had no interest in maintaining Beijing's commitment to the 'one country, two systems' arrangement enshrined in the territory's Basic Law.

In 2019, as European concerns about the CCP's policies mounted, the EU released a carefully crafted new strategy that called China a 'systemic rival', alongside being an economic 'competitor' and a 'cooperation partner' on global challenges like climate change.[8] Although still emphasizing the mutual interest the two sides have in managing the global agenda, the reference to systemic rivalry reflected EU leaders' opposition to China's approach to human rights and international law, and their readiness to pursue more assertive policies towards China in response.

In January 2021, with support for closer economic relations leaching from the European Parliament and EU governments wanting to demonstrate a more coordinated transatlantic approach to China after the election of President Biden, the EU withdrew its plan to ratify the EU–China Comprehensive Agreement on Investment. The two sides had finalized the agreement in December 2020, after seven years of negotiations to improve European access to the still heavily protected Chinese market.

Then, in June 2021, in a major break in their past approach, all EU members plus the UK and Norway joined the US in imposing sanctions on four Chinese CCP officials based in Xinjiang, including the party's second most senior representative, for their treatment of the Uighur population. Beijing immediately retaliated by sanctioning five members of the European Parliament who had consistently challenged China over its human rights violations. It also extended the sanctions to the EU's Political and Security Committee and the Berlin-based MERICS think tank, which had long warned about the risks that a more repressive China posed for Europe. The Europe–China relationship went from fragile to frayed.

Beijing's decision to sanction elected EU representatives and an independent civil society organization crystallized for European leaders the unbridgeable divide between them and China and cemented their tougher line. There is now little chance that the hard-won investment agreement will be resuscitated, all the more so because European companies, which might have once lobbied hard for it, have become increasingly jaded by their experiences in the Chinese market.

Where Volkswagen and German chemicals giant BASF are among the companies that have shored up their commitment to China, many others complain bitterly about China's demands that they transfer their intellectual property (IP) to their Chinese partners as a condition for doing business, and other market-distorting measures that have severely limited their ability to be profitable. In its 2023 Business Confidence Survey, the EU Chamber of Commerce in China noted a significant deterioration in the conditions for European business operating there and that a 'decoupling' of certain business operations was under way.[9] And EU Trade Commissioner Valdis Dombrovskis stated that the ever-widening Chinese trade surplus with the EU, which hit a record €277 billion in 2022, was a sign of Chinese market distortions.[10] The situation threatened to deteriorate further as Chinese electric vehicle production began to swamp the EU market, with the Chinese share growing from near zero in 2021 to 8 per cent in 2022, and estimates this could double to 15 per cent by 2025. On 13 September 2023, the European Commission launched a subsidy investigation which could add another 10 per cent or more to the 10 per cent tariffs already levied on EVs imported from China.[11]

On the back of these steadily worsening economic relations, the CCP's refusal to condemn Russia over its invasion of Ukraine has taken the relationship to a new low and led to the three Baltic states withdrawing from Beijing's prized '17 + 1' forum for economic cooperation with a group of Central and East European countries. Negative public sentiment towards China hit all-time highs in most European countries, ranging between 65 and 80 per cent of those polled, a stark contrast to negative perceptions in the range of 25 to 40 per cent in the early 2000s.[12] Whatever concerns Russia had about Ukraine, nothing, in European eyes, justifies breaking the most fundamental law of the post-war UN-sanctioned order: internationally recognized borders will not be changed by force.

The contradiction between Beijing's assertions that it upholds this order while also supporting Russia's justifications for invasion reminded European leaders that China is just another great power that prizes sovereign action over international law. Where would China stand if Russian forces provoked a separatist incident among Russian communities in one of the Baltic states, as a pretext for an intervention? And what would be its attitude if Russia decided to assert sovereignty over, say, the contested Lomonosov Ridge in the Arctic High North? After the Ukraine invasion, China's illegal occupation of islands in the South China Sea, ignoring the ruling of the Permanent Court of Arbitration on the illegality of their action and then turning them into heavily armed outposts, seems a less distant threat to European policymakers. As are the signs that China is building the capacity to be able to intimidate or even force unification with Taiwan at some point in the near future.

The ambiguity of China's response to Russia's 2022 invasion of Ukraine was also a harsh wake-up call to the fact that Europe cannot afford to be in a dependent or even overly interdependent economic relationship with China. The CCP already has a record of using its growing economic power to show its displeasure with European foreign policy. It threatened British exports and refused any official trade visits after Prime Minister Cameron met the Dalai Lama in the UK in 2012. Norway saw its exports of salmon to China banned after the Nobel Committee awarded the Peace Prize to the Chinese human rights campaigner Liu Xiaobo in 2013. And Lithuanian exports to China were banned in December 2021 after political leaders in Vilnius changed the name of their Taiwan Representation Office. This affected not only exports from Lithuania, but those of other EU member businesses that contained Lithuanian components.

These spats pale into insignificance compared to the new risks to European economic stability due to overdependence on China for the inputs to the green energy transition. Whereas the transition to renewable energy was pressing and important in 2021, since Russia's invasion of Ukraine and the sanctioning or blocking of most of its energy supplies to Europe, it has become urgent and critical. In 2022, however, Europe imported from China 90 per cent of its solar panels or related components, 90 per cent of its processed lithium and other rare earth minerals, and 60 per cent of the components for its wind turbines. European leaders simply cannot afford to convert their countries' ultimately self-harming dependency on Russia for gas supplies into an equally dangerous dependency for their renewable energy inputs on a country – China – with which they have such fundamental policy differences.

The end of Europe's third way

Europe is in the midst of an important transition in its relationship with China. The most recent EU strategy on China, released in June 2023, held the line on the trifecta of China as competitor, partner and systemic rival.[13] But recent and planned European policies show that the view of China as a rival and competitor is now far more pronounced, reflecting the steady deterioration in relations and loss of underlying trust.

For example, European governments plan to join the US in passing legislation that will sanction companies for using forced labour in their supply chains. Although the legislation is not targeted specifically at China, it builds on a 2018 UN report that concluded forced labour was taking place among Uighur, Kazakh and other minorities in the agricultural and manufacturing sectors in Xinjiang. Under the banner of derisking rather than decoupling their economic relationship from China, European governments have passed a series of national laws to impose limits on Chinese investment in sensitive sectors, from critical infrastructure such as telecoms and nuclear energy, to high-technology sectors, such as semiconductor design and quantum computing. The Netherlands has joined the US in banning the export of advanced semiconductor manufacturing equipment to China. The Italian government under Prime Minister Giorgia Meloni has withdrawn Italy from the Memorandum of Understanding (MoU) that her predecessor Giuseppe Conte had signed with China in March 2019 to participate in the Belt and Road Initiative.

Like the US, Europeans are also responding to China's dominance of the green energy sector by ramping up national and EU-level subsidies and grants to build up their own green industries, from battery production and upgrading new interconnectors to electricity grids to mining and processing rare earth minerals. The EU is applying roughly two-thirds of its collective €750 billion post-COVID Recovery and Resilience Facility towards funding the energy transition. And the European Commission has loosened its rules on member states providing national subsidies to assist this process, despite the potentially distortive effects this will have on the EU single market. The German government alone has provided €200 billion in domestic subsidies on everything from households installing new heat pumps instead of gas boilers to convincing foreign semiconductor manufacturers to locate their new plants in Germany – Intel's planned $30 billion fabrication plant in Germany will be one of its largest in the world. And, despite the head start that China has built up in critical mineral investments in Africa, European governments have increased their engagement there markedly since 2020 in order to diversify their supplies, including a new pledge of €150 billion to an 'Africa–EU Investment Package' focused on infrastructure, health and education.[14]

These steps still leave extensive scope for Europe and China to continue trading with each other and investing in each other's economies across a host of less sensitive economic sectors. And European publics appear to still take a pragmatic view of the balance of risks and opportunities.[15] But there is much greater alignment now between European policymakers' approach and that of their US counterparts to the economic relationship with China. And, with Europe more reliant than ever on the United States for its security, its policymakers are likely to keep ratcheting up the limits on Chinese engagement in sensitive sectors in line with Washington if this is the direction that US policymakers choose to take.

Similarly, on the security front, European governments joined the US and Canada to highlight for the first time the challenges China poses to their collective security in NATO's new 2022 Strategic Concept, which harshly condemned China for its 'coercive policies', 'malicious hybrid and cyber operations', 'confrontational rhetoric and disinformation' targeting NATO members, and its efforts to 'control key strategic materials and supply chains'.[16] Individually, between 2020 and 2022, most major European countries – France, Germany, the Netherlands, the UK – issued Indo-Pacific strategies, under which they pledge to increase their military presence across the region and to conduct more military training exercises with regional partners, thereby picking up some of the load from the US. Europeans know that if they are to dispel calls among some US policymakers to shift more of America's defence resources from Europe to the Asia–Pacific region they need to show their counterparts in Washington that they take the China threat seriously and as a collective concern.

Still, as important as these European steps might be, they cannot dispel the underlying concern across Europe that America is now a far less predictable global partner in managing the risks from a rising China. With the 2024 presidential election in the balance and a Republican Party that would likely return to putting America first in its trade and foreign policy, Europeans would benefit from enlarging the group of liberal democracies confronting Russia and China, so they are less dependent on unpredictable US leadership in the New Cold War. Tentative steps in this direction are already taking place.

7

America's Atlantic and Pacific allies converge

One of the defining features of the New Cold War is the emergence of a new, though presently informal, Atlantic–Pacific partnership. For the first time, America's transatlantic allies organized around NATO are interlinking with its main Pacific allies – Australia, Japan and South Korea – through a mix of new security and technological partnerships. The motivations are clear: the US needs a larger group of allies to manage the interrelated threats posed by China and Russia. And America's European and Pacific allies believe that by showing they take both threats equally seriously they will underpin America's commitment to their own regions.

The G7 has emerged as the main forum for coordinating the imposition of sanctions and measures to strengthen the economic and technological security of this group of 'like-minded' countries. But G7 consistency and coherence are still in their infancy, as the US and EU compete to subsidize their new green industries, and America's allies try to avoid being backed by the US into a zero-sum contest with China that would be far more damaging for their economies.

Growing concerns over China among America's Asian allies

As the last Cold War took shape, there were important differences between how America extended its security umbrella to its allies across the Atlantic and those across the Pacific. The US-led Atlantic Alliance was established in 1949 along treaty lines and has elaborate and formal military structures and coordination processes, including an integrated military command, with a US-appointed Supreme Allied Commander and permanent military staff based in Mons, Belgium, reflecting the continuity of US command of allied forces from the end of the Second World War. In the Asia–Pacific region, America's alliances are bilateral and reflect the specific history and circumstances of the US's relationship with each country. In addition, the US troops based in the region have largely remained in place, whereas in Europe most US troops were withdrawn in the two decades after the collapse of the Soviet Union.

Nevertheless, there is a clear parallel between the way that US and European relations with China have deteriorated over the last ten years and the trajectory of the relationship between America's three main Asian allies and China. South Korea, Japan and Australia has each gone from enjoying a heyday of economic opportunity to unease over China's growing influence over regional security, to concern over excessive economic dependence after Xi Jinping's changes to China's political economy. Together, these fears have pushed them closer to the US and to the transatlantic alliance.

South Korea

Given Beijing's long-standing support for the North Korean regime in Pyongyang, South Korean leaders have consistently sought to stay on good terms with China, confident in doing so of their treaty-bound protection by the United States. China has grown to be South Korea's largest trading partner, with trade of over $155 billion in 2022; the US came in second at $110 billion, and others are far behind (Japan was in fourth place with trade of $30 billion).[1] South Korean companies have invested heavily inside China's growing market, using it also as a base from which to acquire at competitive prices the components for their dramatic rise as the most successful east Asian economy after Japan.

But, as Xi has pursued China's territorial claims in the region more aggressively, Seoul has found itself in direct dispute with Beijing as well as in the crossfire between China and Washington. From the early 1990s, China began to challenge South Korea's sovereignty over Ieodo, a submerged rock known internationally as Socotra Rock, in the East China Sea, despite its much closer proximity to South Korea and the existence of a South Korean research centre perched on a platform above it. As with the islands in the South China Sea, the claims matter not only for security, but because they help delineate the limits of each country's special economic zones, which extend 200 nautical miles beyond the nearest land boundary and which can be used to claim rights to crucial mineral resources, including oil and gas.[2]

Washington and Seoul share growing concerns about the reach and lethality of North Korea's nuclear and missile programmes, which Beijing has proven unwilling or unable to curb. In 2016, this led Seoul to deploy the Americans' Terminal High Altitude Area Defense (THAAD) anti-ballistic missile system in South Korea. The CCP saw this deployment as a direct threat to China's own security, as the system could also target Chinese missiles and undermine its nuclear deterrent. It blocked Chinese tourist visits to South Korea which had accounted for nearly half of tourist arrivals that year and over 70 per cent of duty-free sales. It also engineered a comprehensive set of restrictions on the operations of the South Korean conglomerate Lotte Group, which ended up closing 87 of its 112 hypermarkets across China.[3]

In October 2017, the Moon Jae-in presidency sought to placate Beijing by committing itself to the 'three noes': no more additional deployments of THAAD missiles, no participation in a US missile defence system and no formation of a US–Japan–South Korea military alliance. Beijing pocketed President Moon's three noes, while North Korea's nuclear weapons programme continues to expand, including the range and sophistication of its missile delivery systems.

Since his election in March 2022, the conservative President Yoon Suk Yeol has taken a much harder line on China and North Korea and strengthened South Korea's alliance with the US. In August 2022, he restarted the annual large-scale summer military exercise Freedom Shield, which involves 58,000 South Korean and US military personnel simulating a joint response to a North Korean attack. And South Korea hosted a first visit in forty years by a US nuclear ballistic missile submarine to the port of Busan in July 2023.[4] President Yoon even broke a longstanding taboo and criticized Beijing in April that year for threatening peace across the Taiwan Strait.[5]

At the same time, South Korean businesses are reducing their reliance on Chinese-based inputs for critical high-tech exports, including in the field of battery technology.[6] This was partly to make their supply chains more resilient to a future deterioration in US–China relations after the THAAD experience, and partly a response to the inducements contained in the Biden administration's Inflation Reduction Act, which linked access to its subsidies to commitments by recipient countries not to increase levels of investment in China.

The most dramatic step has been President Yoon's agreement, alongside President Fumio Kishida of Japan and President Biden, to sign a new Trilateral Partnership between the three countries at Camp David in August 2023. Although it is not a military alliance, it goes beyond a mere normalization of relations between Seoul and Tokyo, which have been poisoned by the legacy of Japan's annexation of South Korea from 1910 through 1945, and the human rights abuses perpetrated throughout this period. The partnership includes commitments to hold annual meetings of the three countries' leaders and to share intelligence on North Korean missiles tests and offers a real opportunity for the US to build a stronger front against Chinese domination of northeast Asia.[7]

Japan

As a violent aggressor and colonizer of parts of mainland China in the 1930s, Japan has the most fraught relationship with China of any of its neighbours. After Japan surrendered unconditionally in 1945 following the devastation of the American nuclear attacks on Hiroshima and Nagasaki, it adopted a pacifist constitution and imposed strict limits on the purpose and capabilities of its military. Yet these actions have been insufficient to alter the official and popular Chinese narrative that Japan continues to be led by unreconstructed nationalists who have never atoned genuinely for their past misdeeds and who still harbour expansionist ambitions. The association between leaders of Japan's ruling Liberal Democratic Party, including the late Prime Minister Shinzo Abe, and the infamous Yasukuni Shrine outside Tokyo, which houses a memorial to several indicted war criminals, feeds this perception. The CCP is also happy to keep alive the memory of Japan's war crimes and pride in the CCP's role in Japan's defeat as a tool of nationalist cohesion. Chinese TV continues to be awash night after night with historical dramas depicting ruthless Japanese troops brutalizing Chinese citizens during the occupation.

It is all the more remarkable that, since the 1990s, China has grown to be Japan's principal export market, ahead of the US and Germany. And that, until the COVID pandemic, Chinese tourists had grown to be the largest contingent visiting Japan each year, with over 9.5 million in 2019, representing 30 per cent of the total.[8] It is less surprising that, while keeping up a steady rate of investment into China, Japanese companies have been loath to invest as heavily as their South Korean and European counterparts in local production that could compromise Japan's leadership in critical areas of technology and turn China into an even more fearsome competitor than it already is. Nor have Chinese companies become major investors in Japan's industrial or technological base.

As with South Korea, China's growing assertion of what it believes are its territorial rights has brought it into direct contest with Japan. The flashpoint is the small group of five uninhabited islands covering only 7 square kilometres, known in Japan as the Senkakus and in China as the Diaoyu Islands, which lie near Taiwan and the southern part of the Ryukyu island chain, west of Okinawa. These returned to Japanese administration in the Okinawa Reversion Treaty of 1971. China had let its claim to the islands rest until this point, which coincided with a UN report that large oil and gas reserves might exist in their vicinity. But it reacted furiously after the Japanese government formally purchased the islands in 2012 from a family that was planning to sell them to a Japanese nationalist group. Beijing has since stepped up its rate of naval incursions into and aircraft sorties over the waters around the islands, to the point where Chinese Coast Guard vessels now constantly challenge Japan's control of the waters, seeking to demonstrate that they are the ones exercising administrative control of the area.[9]

In response, Japan became one of the countries that is most vocal in criticizing China's illegal occupation of several of the Spratly and Paracel Islands in the South China Sea. And, under Abe's doctrine of 'proactive pacifism', it also began selling significant quantities of defence equipment, including radar systems and patrol boats, to countries contesting China's claims – principally Indonesia, Malaysia, the Philippines and Vietnam – to help them enforce control over their sovereign waters and the islands within them.[10]

Japan's concerns about China's military modernization and more assertive regional behaviour have grown alongside those in Washington. After the election of Donald Trump, Japanese political leaders realized that an increasingly hawkish US would no longer tolerate Japan freeriding on America's security commitment behind its pacifist constitution and keeping its defence spending under 1 per cent of GDP. In his second term as prime minister, Abe secured support for a historic change to the constitution that would permit it to use its self-defence forces to come to the aid of allies under attack; a clear route for Japan to support America should it enter conflict with China in the region.

When Prime Minister Kishida visited President Biden in Washington in May 2022, he became the first Japanese leader to declare publicly the importance of 'peace and stability in the Taiwan Strait'.[11] He then committed in December 2022 to double Japan's defence spending by 2027 to 2 per cent of GDP, which, given the size of its economy, would make it one of the largest defence spenders in the world. In March 2023, the government announced that its new defensive capabilities would include 400 US long-range Tomahawk cruise missiles capable of hitting Chinese missile bases on its mainland.[12] Tokyo also completed the long-delayed process of approving and paying for new bases for the US forces stationed in Okinawa, which is in the middle of the Japan-controlled Ryukyu island chain and whose southernmost island, Yonaguni, lies just seventy miles off the east coast of Taiwan. Should China attempt to take Taiwan by force and the US were to intervene, it seems likely that Japan would be drawn into the conflict.

Australia

Australia's relationship with China has followed a similar trajectory to its northeast Asian neighbours. As with Japan and South Korea, Australia has benefited enormously from China's economic rise. Australia's vast reserves of coal and iron ore powered China's economic growth. In 2022, Australia provided a record 65 per cent of China's imports of iron ore, while China accounted for 30 per cent of Australia's total exports.[13] Through the early 2000s, this significant economic relationship continued to expand and diversify, with Chinese students becoming one of the largest contingents at Australian universities, and Chinese companies making major investments averaging $10 billion per annum from 2011 to 2017, principally in Australian mining operations, with the rest in agriculture and real estate.[14] In 2015, the Northern Territory government even granted a ninety-nine-year lease to the port in Darwin, on Australia's strategically placed north coast, to a Chinese company.[15]

Then the relationship started to sour. In 2017, an Australian Senator was sacked by the Labor Party over links between his pro-China statements and relationship with a wealthy Chinese donor. Separately, Beijing began a concerted push to displace Australian and US influence in South Pacific Island nations, which are critical for Australia's regional security. And then, in response to Prime Minister Scott Morrison's calls in April 2020 and July 2021 for a formal international investigation into the origins of the COVID outbreak, Beijing hit back by informally blocking imports of Australian barley, and adding tariffs on imports of Australian wine and customs bans on imports of Australian lobsters, wheat and wool – although it notably took no action against its imports of Australian commodities. Notwithstanding a subsequent easing of political and trade tensions, and reflecting the new consensus on standing up to China's greater assertiveness, Labor Prime Minister Anthony Albanese signed off a new Defence Strategic Review in April 2023, which commits the country to a strategy of deterrence by denial. This will require close cooperation with the US and regional allies as well as additional defence spending.[16]

The two hemispheres unite

The hardening of these three key countries' bilateral relations with China, after twenty years of focusing on the 'win–win' opportunities emanating from China's rise, has underscored their dependence on the US for protection. Torn between pursuing economic opportunities with their giant neighbour and needing to remain closely connected to the US for their security, the latter is winning out.

Also contributing to this strategic reassessment has been China's deeper alignment with Russia since 2022. Since the end of the Cold War, Japan and South Korea had maintained cordial relations with Moscow. South Korean companies became big exporters and manufacturers of cars and electrical appliances in Russia, importing mostly energy and minerals in return. But, although Russia supplied up to a quarter of Korea's imports of naphtha (an important refined petroleum product) and a quarter of the enriched uranium for its nuclear power plants, its total trade amounted only to £27 billion in 2021, equivalent to 2.2 per cent of its total.[17] The priority has been to remain on good terms with Moscow, lest Russia decides to increase its support for the North Korean regime.

Japanese leaders had their own reasons to sustain good relations with Moscow. Russia is an important source of oil and gas imports, which are essential since the Japanese government closed its nuclear power plants after the Great Eastern Earthquake and tsunami, which led to the Fukushima nuclear disaster in March 2011. Japanese companies hold a big stake in the Sakhalin gas fields just north of the Japanese island of Hokkaido.

The Russian government matters to Tokyo also because Moscow's close relationship with the regime in Pyongyang puts it in a position to check North Korea's provocative missile tests, several of which have overflown Japanese territory. Moreover, Japan has been trying to convince Moscow to enter negotiations that would lead to the return of the Northern Territories, four large islands that Russia seized from Japan at the end of the Second World War. Prime Minister Abe spent much of his second premiership, from 2012 until 2020, hoping to broker a deal with Putin, with whom he met on twenty-seven occasions.

By 2019, however, it was clear that Putin had no intention of negotiating their return.[18] Now, following Russia's invasion of Ukraine and its closer alignment with China, there is zero prospect that Moscow will support progress on the islands or on helping check North Korea's provocative missile launches. Instead, Japan and America's other two main Pacific allies face a clearer choice – rather than trying to straddle the line between depending on the US for their security and prioritizing good economic relations with Beijing and Moscow, they must commit to their security guarantor, distance themselves from Russia and hedge more assiduously against China.

These new geopolitical dynamics have opened the way for one of the most distinctive developments of the New

Cold War: the integration for the first time of America's transatlantic and transpacific alliances. Just as Europeans need to show that they care about the China threat in order to sustain America's commitment to Europe, so America's Pacific allies must show Washington that they care about the Russia threat in order to underpin Washington's commitment to their region.

In April 2022, Japan, South Korea and Australia, along with New Zealand and Singapore, signed up to the suite of transatlantic sanctions against Russia, the first time they had sanctioned the country. Although they are not mirror images of the Western sanctions, they cover the same sectors, including finance, and the three governments have continued to expand and upgrade them in parallel with their Western allies.[19] The prime ministers of all these countries, bar Singapore, attended the June 2022 NATO summit in Madrid, which focused on confronting Russia's aggression as well as highlighting the new security challenges posed by China, and also the 2023 summit in Vilnius that took further steps to counter Russia in the long term.

In September 2020, Australia, the US and the UK first announced a multi-decade AUKUS agreement, under which the three long-standing allies will jointly develop high-end new technologies with military applications, as well as supply by the late 2030s a new nuclear-powered, conventionally armed submarine fleet for the Australian navy. These submarines will enable Australia to join its allies in monitoring and deterring China's growing naval capabilities from the South Pacific to the South China Sea.

In January 2023, Japan signed a Reciprocal Forces Agreement with the UK, enabling the British government to send forces there at short notice.[20] British Typhoon fighters have exercised alongside the Japanese air force and, in the summer of 2021, a UK-led Carrier Strike Group that included US and Dutch air and naval forces in support paid a port visit to Tokyo after sailing there through the South China Sea. Having lost out on a major submarine sale to Australia as a result of AUKUS, France has nevertheless deepened its naval deployments and exercises through the Asia–Pacific. The US and its major Pacific and European allies are all conscious that a large proportion of their seaborne trade flows through the South China and East China Seas and refuse to concede them strategically to China. Japan's 2015 call for a 'free and open Indo-Pacific' has become a rallying mantra for this emerging Atlantic–Pacific community.

Holding the Atlantic–Pacific partnership together

Although there has been no formal agreement linking the major liberal democracies across the Atlantic and Pacific hemispheres, the G7 has emerged as their main coordinating forum to respond to the new threats from China and Russia.

The origins of the G7 go back to 1973 when the US and its closest European allies gathered to discuss their response to the first global oil crisis. By 1977, the group had expanded to its current membership of Canada, France, Germany, Italy, Japan, the UK and the US, with the European Union participating formally from 1981. In 1994, it evolved into the G8 when Russia was invited to join. But Russia was expelled from the group twenty years later, following its annexation of Crimea. In 2022, the G7 accounted for 45 per cent of global GDP and 50 per cent of global defence spending. Although it is a 'non-enumerated member', the EU adds enormously to the global clout of the G7, given its responsibility for coordinating the trade and foreign economic policies of all twenty-seven EU member states, including sanctions.

What began in the late 1970s as a forum for global economic and financial coordination has acquired a much larger remit. Throughout the 1980s, the G7 developed common positions on security challenges such as the Iran–Iraq War and the Soviet occupation of Afghanistan. In the 1990s, its agenda expanded to global debt management, and from the 2000s it has coordinated positions on sustainable development and climate change. There was a period when it looked like the G7 might fall into irrelevance, after the regular meetings of the finance ministers of the world's twenty biggest economies evolved during the global financial crisis of 2008–09 into an annual 'G20 summit', including the EU, to serve as 'the premier coordinating body for international economics'. But the drift into a new Cold War with China and Russia has thrust the G7 back into the foreground.

The G7 now serves as the forum for ensuring consistency between the sanctions packages that are generally developed in Brussels, London, Ottawa and Washington and for coordinating them with Tokyo, Seoul and Canberra. It is where these same capitals coordinate the scope of their growing controls on trade and investment with China and Russia. And it is where officials work together to assess how best to reduce dependence on China for high-tech and green-tech imports and develop new secure supply chains among themselves in sensitive areas such as semiconductors – what US Treasury Secretary Janet Yellen described in 2022 as 'friend-shoring'.[21]

When the UK held the G7 presidency in 2021, Prime Minister Boris Johnson pushed to expand the club to include formally Australia, India and South Korea. But the preference of current members has been to retain the enlarged group's informality. As it is, sustaining effective coordination and common approaches among the original G7, never mind a new G7+ group of countries including Australia and South Korea, has been difficult. Domestic economic pressures can undermine cooperation, as has become apparent as the US and EU compete over investment in green technologies. Even among these 'like-minded states', cultural and political differences can create obstacles. US and European approaches to data sharing are a perennial bone of transatlantic contention. And it was only after lengthy pressure from US officials that Japanese and South Korean officials came to agreement in June 2023 to reinstate each other as preferred trading destinations and re-establish intelligence sharing, and for Japan to lift its export ban on certain critical minerals to South Korea (all of which had been suspended as a result of an escalation in 2019 of the extant dispute over Japanese abuse of South Korean women during their occupation).[22] Above all, America's Pacific allies, like their European counterparts, remain nervous about being backed by the US too quickly into economic confrontation with China, given the greater relative importance of their economic relationships with their giant neighbour.

Nevertheless, the actions of Russia and China in the past decade have created an unprecedented level of shared purpose among this group of countries. And their mutual reliance on each other for their security in the face of a more aligned China–Russia axis creates a strong impulse for sustained cooperation.

The biggest challenges to the ability of a US-led Atlantic–Pacific partnership grouped around the G7 to influence the outcome of the New Cold War might come from a different direction: the growing economic and diplomatic power of the Global South. This large grouping of countries now has a magnetic geopolitical pull they did not have when many of them gathered under the banner of the Non-Aligned Movement.

8

The non-aligned are now the majority and finding their voice

While America and its allies today make up a declining 50 per cent of global GDP and a shrinking 14 per cent of the world's total population, what was a marginal Non-Aligned Movement of seventy-seven countries (G77) in the last Cold War is now nearly double that number. Together, they constitute a growing 65 per cent of world population – including some of the world's most populous nations such as India, Indonesia, Nigeria and Brazil – and nearly 30 per cent of world GDP. (China is included on the latest list of the G77 but was not involved in its creation and does not consider itself a member.)

The one thing that unites all these countries is their refusal to accept that their futures and the world's will be framed by a new Cold War in which, once again, they have no voice. Their leaders reject being bit players in a contest between the leading authoritarian and democratic powers and see no need to be loyal to those that match their own forms of political governance. Instead, they are taking advantage of opportunities to strengthen their economies and their security by triangulating between

China and Russia, on the one hand, and the US and its allies, on the other.

The evolution of the Non-Aligned Movement

In the last Cold War, members of the Non-Aligned Movement hoped to pursue an independent future, free from the dominant competition between the US and the Soviet Union. Many of them had secured their sovereignty or self-determination only in the 1950s and 1960s, as the British and other European empires retreated under the financial stress of post-war economic reconstruction at home and pressure from Soviet-backed national uprisings abroad.

But these countries quickly discovered that their influence over their futures, never mind the direction of the Cold War that defined the global context in which they existed, was next to nil. Their economies were too small and disparate to create an alternative economic pole and insufficiently developed to enable them to set their own terms of trade. In the 1980s, average real incomes across the G77 were a seventh that of developed OECD countries.[1] And their lack of military capability meant they were consumers of the international security environment rather than contributors to it. At various points, proxy wars between the US and Soviet Union blighted sub-Saharan Africa, Latin America, the Middle East, South Asia and Southeast Asia; whether it involved the superpowers funding full-blown insurgencies (as in Angola or Nicaragua) or, as was more often the case, backing loyal regimes against an opposition whose rise to power might shift, however marginally, the balance of regional power in favour of the other side. This was the logic for the US backing military juntas in Argentina, Chile and Pakistan and, later, autocratic leaders in Egypt and Saudi Arabia – and for the Soviets backing their client governments in Cuba, Ethiopia, Nicaragua and Syria.

Again, this time things are different. First of all, the number of countries in the world has grown following further steps towards national self-determination and the collapse of the Soviet Union. There were 154 members of the UN in 1980, at the height of the Cold War, and 195 by 2023. Second, given improvements in pre- and post-natal care alongside the demographic ageing of Europe, their share of the world population has exploded. The population of those non-aligned countries reached some 5 billion people, of a world total of just over 8 billion, in 2023.

Third, following thirty years of US-led economic globalization and ten years with the added stimulus of massive Chinese investment in global commodity and infrastructure projects, the relative economic weight of the non-aligned countries is growing. The countries of Southeast Asia have been the main success story to date. But India's share of the global economy is projected to grow rapidly in the coming decades, overtaking the EU in 2050 on its way to being the world's second or third largest economy alongside the US and China later this century.[2] The Gulf states are investing their wealth more strategically than in the past, turning this region into the main hub for trade involving emerging economies. There has been an important shift in patterns of world trade; so-called South–South trade expanded from 17 per cent of the total in 2005 to 28 per cent in 2021, partly on the back of the increasing importance of commodity exports to feed China's growth.[3]

Countries in Latin America and sub-Saharan Africa, however, continue to struggle to achieve sustainable growth, as witnessed, for example, by the severe economic setbacks in countries such as Argentina, Ghana and Zambia, in recent years, and persistent instability in Libya, Somalia, Sudan, Haiti and most of Central America. Bad governance, state capture by kleptocratic elites – often enabled by private Western intermediaries as well as official Russian or Chinese support – and ethnic and religious violence all continue to blight much of the Global South. Their collective voice and political clout in the international institutions that write the rules of today's international order remain small.

But, as their share of global trade and the global economy grows, so does their potential value to the two sides of the new geopolitical divide. The result is that, at the very least, the non-aligned countries are in a far stronger position than in the last Cold War; they can triangulate between the two sides to try to secure national advantage.

New opportunities to triangulate

India is playing its hand particularly well. Although it is the world's largest democracy, it refuses to be co-opted by the US or its European allies into aligning itself only with the democratic side of the divide. Rather than join them in sanctioning Russia for its invasion of Ukraine, it has taken advantage of Russia's need to find new markets for its oil exports and increased its imports tenfold since mid-2022. In addition, it has used a portion of these imports to become a principal exporter of refined oil to Europe and other Western markets which have banned direct imports of these products from Russia.[4] It also continues to import arms from Russia, which has been its largest supplier since the early years of the last Cold War, accounting for 65 per cent of its total imports from 2013–17, although its share has fallen to 45 per cent in the period 2018–22 as a result of competition from the US and France, even before the pressure on Russian arms exports being exerted by the need to service the invasion of Ukraine.[5]

For New Delhi, this is a logical and straightforward decision. America has long bankrolled and supplied advanced weapons to Pakistan, even when it was under military rule, which has harboured Islamist terrorists who have carried out violent attacks inside India, including an assault on the Indian parliament in December 2001 that left nine dead, and an even more lethal attack in November 2008 on the Taj Mahal Palace hotel and other locations in Mumbai which killed 175 civilians. In contrast, Russia has been a reliable supplier of advanced weapons that have been essential for India to protect itself not only against Pakistan but also against its main rival, China.

India harbours profound concerns about China's economic and military rise and its aggressive efforts in recent years to change the disputed border between the two countries, known as the Line of Actual Control. The Modi government was prepared, therefore, to accept the invitation from the Biden team in September 2021 to elevate the 'Quad' forum from ministerial to summit-level meetings between the leaders of Australia, India, Japan and the US. They now coordinate their efforts on a broad range of areas of soft security, from joint naval patrols to combat piracy and illegal fishing to the development of new vaccines to manage a future pandemic.[6]

New Delhi's promiscuous foreign policy has worked to its advantage. The US is increasing the sophistication of the armaments it sells to India, announcing the sale of fighter jet engines, precision-guided missiles and long-range drones during Modi's state visit to the United States in June 2023.[7] It also continues to help it build the capability to enrich uranium for its civilian nuclear programme domestically. For their part, despite their staunch support for Ukraine, the EU and UK are making a concerted effort to complete free trade agreements with India.

The Kingdom of Saudi Arabia, America's traditional ally in the Gulf, is following a similar playbook to India. Under the ambitious and ruthless leadership of Crown Prince Mohammed bin Salman, Saudi Arabia has pivoted from being a loyal follower of the US to a country with a far more independent foreign policy. In late 2016, it expanded the OPEC oil cartel that it leads to include Russia and nine other non-OPEC oil producing countries, creating the so-called 'OPEC+'. Under its aegis, Saudi Arabia now coordinates oil production levels closely with Moscow, despite the latter's invasion of Ukraine, even going against the Biden administration's explicit request in the summer of 2022 to increase production and thereby reduce prices following the invasion.

At the same time Saudi Arabia has been deepening its relations with Beijing. In March 2023, it accepted Chinese mediation to broker a return to diplomatic relations with Iran, despite the ongoing expansion of Iran's stocks of highly enriched uranium, following the collapse in 2017 of the Obama-era agreement to restrict them. With China now the principal recipient of Saudi Arabian oil, Mohammed bin Salman is also engaging Chinese companies closely in his Vision 2030 plan to transform the Kingdom into a more diversified economy, using many of the Chinese companies that Washington has blocked from accessing US markets and technology. He is also investing some of Saudi Arabia's newly burgeoning hard currency reserves into Chinese companies involved in the high-technology race with America, including in AI.[8]

Other countries are gaining greater agency in the New Cold War, including Turkey and Brazil. Turkey is a NATO member that has been an important supplier of weaponry to Ukraine. But this has not stopped President Erdoğan from greatly expanding the country's trading relationship with Russia since the outbreak of the war, while at the same time demanding that the EU reopen negotiations on its accession in return for Ankara's support for Finland and Sweden's accession to NATO. President Lula da Silva of Brazil considers himself a bulwark of democracy against the populist authoritarian threat from his most recent predecessor, President Jair Bolsonaro. Yet China is now by far the largest importer of Brazil's agricultural exports, and Lula has made deepening Brazil's economic relations with China and working with it to design alternatives to US economic dominance two of his main foreign policy priorities.[9]

Setting their own course

This newfound leverage could prove fleeting unless the non-aligned countries can harness it to longer-term progress. Most of them still suffer from significant and, in some cases, structural internal limitations. Despite India's enormous economic potential, it continues to be hampered by its fragmented federal political system, gaps in energy and transport infrastructure, a small middle class, opaque business practices, and a suspicion of foreign investment. Saudi Arabia is still a long way from diversifying its economy successfully from its dependence on fossil fuels. All need to invest more in their public health and in the quality of their education. Triangulation is only valuable if these countries can take control of their economic destinies more broadly and reduce their dependence on the developed world.

Saudi Arabia and India are trying to do this. India has invested heavily in its broadband infrastructure in recent years. It now has some 800 million active internet users, well over half its population, and the government is rolling out impressive new digital tools to deliver its services to citizens more efficiently.[10] Saudi Arabia is opening itself to Chinese 5G and other technologies in order to accelerate its modernization and urbanization, refusing US demands not to partly because of the speed with which its leadership wants to move.

Many of the non-aligned countries are also taking a leaf out of the big powers' own histories of industrialization and building a protected home market to force domestic companies and foreign investors to lift the country up the economic value chain, whereby they manufacture and even export their own high-value products, rather than importing them. For example, India and Saudi Arabia are leveraging competition between the US and China to secure greater investment in their own defence industries, rather than only buying in new equipment from the US, Europe and Russia. Indonesia and Chile have introduced limits on exports of raw lithium from their countries and are instead investing in domestic processing so they can export the more expensive refined product. Indonesia has gone a step further and is now providing incentives for car manufacturers to build electric vehicles there.[11]

African countries are potentially in a strong position, given their reserves of minerals that are essential to the transition to more renewable forms of energy, and the fact that China had the strategic foresight to commit itself to investing in accessing these resources early. The US and its European allies are now desperately trying to catch up, giving African governments and companies much greater influence on the terms of foreign investment decisions.

Southeast Asian countries have their own opportunity. Chinese companies and foreign investors, especially G7-based companies, are shifting some of their manufacturing production out of China and into neighbouring countries so as to benefit from cheaper labour costs and also to be able to continue servicing export markets in the event of a serious deterioration in US–China relations. Vietnam and Malaysia have been among the biggest beneficiaries of this 'China plus one' or 'China plus two' strategy. Policymakers in New Delhi are hoping that the same dynamic will lead major US and other global technology companies to shift some of their China-based supply chains to India. Incredibly, in 2023 Apple still manufactured over 95 per cent of its iPhones, iPads and iMacs in China.[12]

Non-aligned countries are imitating the big powers in other ways. They are building new regional trade groupings that offer beneficial access to their and their neighbours' markets on a regionally reciprocal basis. The ten members of the Association of Southeast Asian Nations (ASEAN) continue their slow but steady process of 'consensus-based' market opening, with the combined market now constituting $3.6 trillion in combined GDP and projected to grow at over 4.5 per cent in 2023. Fourteen Pacific Rim nations joined Japan to complete the Comprehensive and Progressive Trans-Pacific Partnership after the US withdrew from the negotiations in 2017. And African nations finally ratified the African Continental Free Trade Area in 2019, starting the process of reducing tariff barriers to trade between fifty-four countries and three regional economic groupings.

But there is still a long way to go: Latin America's patchwork of old trade agreements, from Mercosur to the Andean Pact, remain fragmented and half-formed; the Gulf Cooperation Council has taken a step backwards since Saudi Arabia introduced new barriers to trade with its Gulf neighbours in July 2021, to try to force more foreign investment into the Kingdom. Meanwhile, neighbours Morocco and Algeria retain extensive obstacles to regional trade and investment as a result of their long-standing dispute over the status of Western Sahara.

And while the New Cold War has empowered the non-aligned countries in the near term, it might prove counterproductive in the longer term for several reasons. The first is that if the contest were to escalate in the future into war, then the scope for triangulation would evaporate. G7 supply chains would need to be devoid of Chinese or Russian inputs, making many companies' 'China plus one' strategies, which often retain supply links back into China, redundant. Indian manufacturing exports to the

US that benefit from Russian energy in their production could become subject to punitive restrictions. And targeted derisking would become broad economic decoupling overnight, leaving many non-aligned economies high and dry, while the protagonists of the New Cold War could fall back on large national markets and protected supply chains.

The next is that there are at least two countries that are ready to use the opportunities to triangulate between the big powers in order to disrupt the status quo. The leaderships in Tehran and Pyongyang reject and seek to undermine the security orders in their regions; North Korea builds ever more destabilizing categories of illegal nuclear weapons, and Iran tries to undermine US influence in the Middle East, including by instigating violent attacks against America's principal regional ally, and Tehran's mortal enemy, Israel. Kim Jong Un's visit to Russia in September 2023 to try to secure even more sophisticated weaponry, and Iran's backing for the terrorist atrocities committed by Hamas against Israeli civilians on 7 October 2023, are signals that intensified geopolitical division has given both sets of leaders a sense of impunity that they did not enjoy before.

The third reason is that there is one giant global challenge – climate change – in the face of which cooperation between the Global South and the Global North will be indispensable. But this cooperation could now prove much harder to achieve, meaning its impacts could be much more devastating, especially for poorer countries.

9

The fight against climate change gets even harder

The first Cold War dominated the global agenda during the second half of the twentieth century. Its features included a massive military stand-off in Europe between the Warsaw Pact and NATO; the constant spectre of nuclear Armageddon; and a series of proxy wars across the world, which contributed to violence and economic insecurity for those outside the protective umbrella of the two superpowers.

The New Cold War threatens to be a dangerous obstacle to global cooperation in confronting another very different and more probable Armageddon, which barely featured on the international agenda prior to 1990. If the world breaches 2°C of global warming above pre-industrial levels in the next two decades, this will trigger catastrophic environmental damage and extreme weather events, potentially leading to a collapse in living standards for much of the world and new outbreaks of strife and instability.

Halting man-made global warming will ultimately depend as much on decisions taken in New Delhi, Cairo, Lagos or Brasilia, where governments must manage still growing populations, and newly industrializing economies, as in Beijing, Washington and Brussels, where combining continued growth with the transition to renewable power is already financially as well as technically feasible. For governments in the Global South, rapid improvement in the prosperity of their relatively poorer populations is the understandable near-term priority. To achieve this in an environmentally sustainable way will require the self-interested support of the richer countries in the Global North. The question is whether they will offer this support, or whether their growing geopolitical and ideological struggles will prevent them from living up to their responsibilities.

The truth hits home

As the 2000s unfolded, so did a growing awareness that the amazing human progress enabled by economic globalization came with severe downsides. Some of these were local – pollution, destruction of flora, fauna and biodiversity. But one stood out above all: warming caused by ever-rising, human-engineered carbon emissions, which leads to dangerous changes in the global climate.

There is no doubt that human activity is driving rising global temperatures and changes to established climate patterns. For two millennia up to the beginning of the Industrial Revolution in 1800, the average amount of carbon dioxide in the atmosphere was 280 parts per million (ppm). Since, it has been on an initially slow and then, from the 1950s, a rapid escalation, reaching a record level of 424 ppm in 2023 – 50 per cent higher than pre-industrial levels.[1] With the rise in carbon emissions comes a rise in global temperatures; scientific models first predicted this in 1896 using knowledge of the greenhouse effect caused by carbon trapped in the Earth's atmosphere.[2]

There are multiple drivers and feedback loops that have accelerated this process. Generating electricity to power industry and people's homes by burning carbon-emitting fossil fuels such as coal, oil and gas is the leading driver. Using oil to power private and public transportation is another. The industrialization of agriculture has led to mass deforestation, reducing the Earth's capacity to process carbon into oxygen, as well as releasing more greenhouse gases from burning the trees, tilling the soil and rearing cattle on the cleared land. The global rise in wealth also helps drive global warming. Demand for higher protein diets with more meat leads to more farming-intensive activity. Greater disposable income increases demand for private transport by land and by air, most of it powered by fossil fuels.

But the feedback loops themselves are an important accelerant. Hotter temperatures increase the demand for air conditioning and refrigeration, which is still delivered mostly by fossil-fuel-powered energy. Warmer oceans absorb less of the carbon we produce, exacerbating the greenhouse effect. Warmer winters mean less ice cover builds up during the colder months at the North and South poles, which then reflect less heat from the sun back into space.

Global warming is already 1.1°C above pre-industrial levels, and the impacts are painfully visible.[3] The five years spanning 2019–23 have been the hottest recorded since the end of the Ice Age. This has led to unprecedented levels of drought, forest fires and floods, record amounts of melting ice sheets at the two poles and bleached coral at the world's reefs. If we breach 2°C of global warming above pre-industrial levels, as we will do by 2050 on our current trajectory, it will trigger catastrophic environmental damage, leading to a collapse of agriculture and fisheries in many parts of the world and extreme weather events, whose costs could lead to a fall in living standards globally. As insects and viruses spread to warmer climates in the north, this could contribute to the rise of new diseases, which could eventually mutate into pandemics. In the most stressed societies, drastic climate change could lead to new civil and inter-state wars, as well as triggering mass migration.[4]

Climate change is a systemic problem that does not respect international boundaries and affects all countries in the world. It will require a system-level response to which all countries contribute. Given the collective benefits from action and the collective costs of inaction, as well as the interconnected nature of the necessary solutions, the response must be coordinated globally with the costs shared equitably. Equitably because the solutions should take into account the principle of 'climate justice'. Those who have historically contributed the most to increased levels of carbon in the atmosphere should logically pay more of the cost, not least because they have become richer faster as a result of their actions. It is patently not fair to expect developing countries that are both poorer and less responsible for global warming to pay equally for a problem they did not create.[5]

All in it together

The good news is that the solutions are available and will be affordable. According to the International Renewable Energy Agency, between 2010 and 2019, the average unit costs globally of installed solar power fell by 85 per cent, for wind energy by 55 per cent, and for lithium-ion batteries by 85 per cent, making them cheaper – once installed – than both gas and coal. Once this cheaper renewable power also charges most vehicles, it will reduce emissions from private transport. Improvements in energy efficiency and the cost-effective development of new technologies, from new battery storage technologies to green hydrogen, could enable the world to keep global warming below 2°C.

The bad news is that the transition will be economically painful for everyone in the near term. Almost all developed and middle-income countries have built their energy and transport infrastructure around fossil power, so there will need to be massive, costly investment in new energy infrastructure, electricity grids, battery storage and charging points. Jobs will be lost alongside the new ones created, but not necessarily at the same time or in the same places.

Countries that have relied heavily on income from national oil and gas companies to feed their government budgets – Russia, Venezuela, the Gulf and some Central Asian states, for example – will see this income shrink and may find it is irreplaceable, creating social and political tensions, unless they can create equally profitable markets for inputs into renewable energy. Developing countries in Latin America and Africa that are only now starting to tap into their significant reserves of oil and gas will find that the markets for them dry up, depriving them of much-needed near-term growth. In the meantime, unlike wealthier countries, they will lack the resources to install and maintain modern renewable energy grids, leaving much of their populations trapped in poverty.

All countries have an interest, therefore, in cooperating to build a predictable, mutually reinforcing energy transition that continues to deliver improvements in standards of living while making economic growth environmentally sustainable.

Between 2000 and 2015, at least, it was not fanciful to believe that governments around the world would come together to pursue this goal. It was an era in which most governments could foresee absolute gains in their international economic relations; another country's gain could also be theirs. The main international security risk during those years was international terrorism. The 9/11 attacks provoked strategic overreach by the US and its allies in Afghanistan and Iraq, including an ill-conceived 'war on terror'. But all governments were united in wanting to defeat international terrorism, as proved by the mix of countries cooperating to combat terrorist financing since September 2001 and in the coalition to defeat Daesh/ISIS, first formed in 2014.

The same sense of shared mission applied to other global challenges, such as preventing the spread of HIV/AIDS, TB and malaria and led to the landmark agreements to achieve the Millennium Development Goals between 2000 and 2015 and then the successor Sustainable Development Goals (SDGs). Formulated by the UN General Assembly in 2015 for completion, in most cases, by 2030, all countries committed to fund or otherwise support the achievement of measurable progress towards seventeen goals, ranging from higher rates of education for young women to universal access to public health and promoting renewable energy.

One of the multilateral agreements that represented the heyday of the 'win–win' approach to international relations was the Paris Agreement to combat climate change, which was finalized at the COP21 summit hosted by the French government in 2015. Operating under the umbrella of the UN's Framework Convention on Climate Change, all countries committed to keep the global average temperature rise this century to no more than 2°C and ideally only 1.5°C above pre-industrial levels by reducing their net carbon emissions to zero by 2050. Reflecting the sensitivity and enormity of this task for all governments, the agreement is not legally binding and there is no enforcement mechanism. Instead, each country makes 'nationally determined contributions' (NDCs) towards achieving this goal. Xi Jinping underscored this fact when he stated that, 'the method, pace and intensity to achieve this goal should and must be determined by ourselves, and will never be influenced by others', a sentiment shared by many in the US Congress.[6]

Nevertheless, all signatories committed to publish how they would achieve their national contributions to the goal of 'net zero', ushering an important level of transparency around each country's process of decarbonizing their national economy and a tool by which governments abiding by the agreement could shame those that did not into living up to their pledges. Subsequent COPs have added more clarity to the road to net zero – targeting coal usage and methane emissions, and publishing mid-term carbon reduction targets. With the Paris framework in place, most businesses have begun their own process to reduce their and their suppliers' carbon footprints towards the 2050 goal.

Progress in reducing greenhouse gas (GHG) emissions by the major emitters has been uneven since 2015 and sets the scene for difficult negotiations ahead. China has become by far the largest emitter of carbon in the world, accounting for 29.2 per cent of total global GHGs in 2022, nearly three times the US at 11.2 per cent. Even considering the fairer measure of GHG emissions per capita, Chinese emissions have been on a rapid rise, exceeding those of the EU27 countries in 2019. At 11 tonnes of CO_2 per capita in 2022, it is still well below the US level of 18 tonnes. However, the US level is falling (from 24 tonnes per capita in 2005), whereas China's is still rising, if now modestly. And, significantly, China's cumulative emissions since the industrial era in 1851 (14.2 per cent of the world total) were almost equal to the EU27's (15.6 per cent) in 2021, making it the third largest cumulative contributor. India's emissions per capita, in contrast, have risen only from 1.6 tonnes per capita in 1990 to 2.8 tonnes in 2022, and it has contributed just 4.6 per cent to the cumulative total so far.[7]

With only twenty-five years to go before the Paris target should be met, the world has now entered the critical phase. Major governments should be coming together to create the conditions within which their countries can drive a comprehensive response. But the rate at which the level of global carbon emissions continues to rise shows that they are not stepping up to the challenge.

Geopolitics and fighting climate change do not mix

Tragically, countries are now finding it harder to cooperate to deal with this global emergency. The transition to a new Cold War is swamping the limited political bandwidth of governments in the Global North that are already struggling to address the worries about economic insecurity accompanying globalization. This is pushing the long-term priority of reducing carbon emissions on to the back burner and bringing the immediate priority of competing with their geopolitical and ideological rivals to the foreground, raising the question of whether they can take on both challenges at the same time. We may have re-entered a period of zero-sum thinking, whereby leaders measure the value of a policy by the extent to which it strengthens or weakens their country relative to their rivals. Societies have tended to tolerate economic hardship for extended periods only in times of war, or during other moments of national crisis, not in return for a long-term vision of climate justice that might benefit others more.

A return to this mindset is reassuring for some political leaders. As Putin has demonstrated, the narrative that a country is in a life-or-death struggle with its ideological enemy can give a leader a clear goal around which to mobilize political support and resources. Unlike climate change, geopolitical rivals are tangible. They exist within a physical territory. The threat they pose is visible, in the shape of missiles, ships and tanks, or at least attributable, if the threat takes the form of a cyber attack or a disinformation operation.

Whereas rewriting internal political bargains to respond to climate change can divide societies internally, a Cold War helps leaders rally their populations around the national flag and strengthen their levers of domestic control. It helps them reinforce their national identity and the narratives that sustain it by defining the enemy as a caricature – the militaristic, bullying Americans; the privileged Europeans still living off their colonial heritage; the soulless Chinese communists for whom individual lives are secondary to the survival of the party; the brutal and amoral Russians.

This brings us to the next problem. The reason many people refuse to accept the evidence of climate change or the human contribution to global warming is not so much that they doubt the science, as that they reject the solutions. They resent having to change their way of life to a low-carbon alternative, or the idea that their governments will have to give up a portion of their sovereignty to pursue internationally mandated targets that might benefit their foreign rivals. This is why climate change could easily become another area of contest in the New Cold War, especially if some democratic governments believe they are simply shifting their energy dependency from one geopolitical rival (Russia and OPEC+), for their oil and gas, to another (China) for their critical minerals and renewable energy.

With Russia on the back foot strategically in Ukraine, the climate emergency offers its leadership an opportunity to sow discontent and disunity among its opponents. The Kremlin can try to undermine the energy transition by provoking instability in countries that will supply the minerals for renewable energy. It has a new popular grievance around which to spread disinformation and political division among the liberal democracies. It can support anti-green political groups, as it did with the anti-vaccine movement during the height of the COVID pandemic.

In China, the transition to a new Cold War increases the pressure on the CCP to confirm the legitimacy of its party rule. The energy transition away from imported fossil fuels will make China more secure in the long term, but in the near term it needs to diversify its imports of oil and gas towards the least vulnerable sources, which lie in Russia, and ensure it controls ports and sea routes for the rest. And, with the US and its allies focusing on economic tools of statecraft to try to contain, or at least to slow, China's rise, there is even less incentive to be transparent about the internal workings of the domestic economy, putting the data that China releases about its achievements to reduce its greenhouse gas emissions in doubt.

European leaders have one thing in common with their Chinese counterparts: concern about energy security now competes with their commitment to climate security. Germany has resumed its coal production to mitigate the fall in Russian gas supply, while the Sunak government has approved new licences to drill for 'British' oil and gas in the North Sea.[8] The extent to which the two sides in the New Cold War can address climate change is predicated on the protagonists accelerating their transitions to renewable energy as a core element of their future energy security. But they are likely to do so more in competition than in cooperation with each other, turning the contest for critical minerals into a mirror image of the contest for oil during the last Cold War.

Getting the priorities right

Political leaders in the Global South are distinctly unimpressed by the excitement among some politicians and analysts in the Global North about the mobilizing impact of a new Cold War for America's alliances. Rather than perceiving this as a welcome commitment by them to uphold the vision of a liberal international order, they resent the revival of a twentieth-century contest between the great powers that could relegate them once again to the status of spectators. They are deeply frustrated that they might remain forever the poorer cousins, as countries in the Global North bring up the economic drawbridge to globalization under the guise of derisking their economies and husband the privileges of being the industrial and technological first movers, often at the south's expense, rather than sharing them for mutual benefit.

One target of their anger is the EU's decision to impose a new carbon tariff (the Carbon Border Adjustment Mechanism, CBAM), as of 2026, on imports that are manufactured in countries that allow higher fossil fuel content than in Europe. This makes sense from a European perspective. Keeping manufacturing industry in Europe is as important politically as it is economically, and European businesses might choose to leave if they have no protection from cheaper imports from countries still using fossil fuels.

In Moscow and Beijing, the CBAM is seen as another weapon in the West's toolbox of geo-economic warfare.[9] But countries in the Global South that are only now developing competitive manufacturing industries have a different complaint: they refuse to accept that, having built their economies on fossil fuels, Europeans should have the right now to punish other countries for doing the same thing.[10] All the more so since Europe, the US and other developed economies missed the goal they set themselves in 2009 and reconfirmed in Paris in 2015 to provide, collectively by 2020, $100 billion per year to finance the less developed economies in adapting to climate change and mitigating its effects. As of November 2023, it was still uncertain whether they had met their target.[11]

G7 governments could argue that they no longer have the financial means to meet their climate pledges in full, in the wake of the very costly COVID pandemic. But this argument does not hold when we consider that in 2022 the US committed $370 billion over the next ten years for its green energy subsidies, the EU committed €750 billion on its post-COVID, green energy recovery through to 2027; Germany found an additional €200 billion for its own national adjustment to higher energy costs after the invasion of Ukraine, plus a commitment of €100 billion extra for its defence budget over the next five years; and the US and Europe between them provided just under $100 billion for the Ukrainians to defend their country in 2022–23 alone.[12] Rather than treating the climate emergency as an opportunity for collective action, countries in the Global South see it as another example of the Global North's attitude of 'us first', despite being the instigators of the planet's changing climate.

The zero-sum thinking that dominates policymaking when governments believe they are in a global contest for survival is the antithesis of the mentality that needs to prevail if countries face shared challenges. But if liberal democracies cannot help poorer countries to address and adapt to climate change, Brazilian leaders will find it hard to argue at home that they should protect rather than exploit the Amazon, despite it being a critical component of global carbon sequestration. Gulf countries and the most efficient Latin American oil and gas producers will intensify their competition to be the long-term suppliers of oil into global markets. And the liberal democracies will end up having to deal with the consequences of runaway planetary warming. More countries in the Sahel and sub-Saharan Africa will fall prey to Russian geopolitical kleptocracy. The Kremlin will be further incentivized to control global food security and insecurity, as energy loses some of its value as an instrument of statecraft.[13] And struggling governments in the Global South will be unable to prevent a mass migration by their populations to the Global North, as sustainable liveli-hoods at home become untenable.

The climate emergency reveals the difficulties of pursuing collective action in a new period of Cold War competition. The institutions that were built at the end of the Second World War to encourage multilateral action on shared challenges and to help deliver peace are strug-gling once again to live up to their mission. Are there complementary or alternative international institutions that can help?

10

The end of multilateralism

The climate emergency underscores the essential need for greater international cooperation this decade. But the deep and mutual suspicion between China and Russia on the one side, and the US and its allies on the other, is leading again to gridlock in the institutions that were established at the end of the Second World War to help countries keep the peace and come together to manage shared challenges.

At the heart of the idea of multilateral cooperation lies the United Nations – along with the specialized international institutions that operate under its aegis, such as the International Monetary Fund (IMF), World Bank and World Health Organization (WHO). For all their faults, these institutions dominated the international landscape during the last Cold War, but each is now struggling to tackle the problems for which they were designed.

Rather than remaining loyal to a slow and sometimes gridlocked UN system, which requires consensus among increasingly diverse, vocal and divided constituents to achieve progress, the New Cold War is driving its protagonists and countries in the Global South to pursue alternative avenues for international cooperation. The US and China are building up clubs of like-minded countries to promote their interests. And the more empowered countries of the Global South are teaming up with them in a plethora of forums to try to manage the international challenges to their prosperity and security in ways that reflect their interests more closely than in the past. Given the impact that challenges such as climate change, pandemic preparedness and food security have on their futures, they refuse to sit on the sidelines.

The international system we have inherited

The United Nations is a remarkable organization, born out of the determination of the victors of the Second World War to create a world body that would promote international peace and prosperity, and prevent a return to the horrors of global conflict that had blighted the first half of the twentieth century. The UN mirrored in many ways the League of Nations, which came into being in January 1920, after the end of the First World War. It too has two decision-making chambers and adopted the League's approach to preventing conflict, with a remit that extends beyond conflict prevention to labour rights, access to public health and protection of minorities, among other topics.

But the UN is shorn of the utopian thinking that contributed to the League's failure in two very important ways. The League's Covenant obliged its members to treat an attack on the territorial integrity of another member as an attack on themselves and to come to its assistance, under the principle of collective security. Once this commitment was tested and found wanting in the 1930s, as fascist Italy and then Nazi Germany began their wars of aggression, the League folded. The UN Charter forbids its members from carrying out wars of conquest or aggression but, apart from permitting states to defend themselves, it passes to the UN Security Council the authority to decide whether member states will challenge the aggression militarily, or economically, or not at all. And, while the League's Council operated by unanimity, the UN Charter gives each of the five permanent members of the UN Security Council – China, France, Russia, the UK and the US; the victors of the Second World War – the right to veto any UN Security Council Resolution, including one to intervene in response to an aggression.

This arrangement helped secure the participation of the US, whose Senate refused to ratify joining the League. But it also creates the impression that the fundamental purpose of the UN Security Council is to prevent war between the great powers, at the expense, if needs be, of aggression against weaker countries, whether perpetrated by the permanent members themselves or their allies.

The UN's record on peace and security has reflected this realist compromise. During the last Cold War, the Korean War of 1950–53 was one of the few major cases where the UN members came together to defend a member state against aggression. But approval was only secured because the Chinese seat in the UN Security Council was at that time held by the nationalist Kuomintang government based in Taiwan, and the Russians were boycotting the UN in opposition. In contrast the UN played no role in the 1962 Sino-Indian war and only a marginal role in the Vietnam War. And subsequently its peacekeeping forces only managed to keep uneasy peace in frozen conflicts from Lebanon to Israel-Palestine.

Similarly, the signing of the nuclear Non-Proliferation Treaty in 1968 is heralded as one of the UN's great successes. But, by designating only the permanent members of the UN Security Council as 'recognized nuclear powers', it further entrenched their privileged position in the new international order. While it is arguable that their possession of nuclear weapons has so far played a role in preventing a new world war, it has not prevented several other states from acquiring nuclear weapons since then.

The UN has proved more successful on the economic

front. Its two main economic agencies, the IMF and the World Bank, supported post-war economic reconstruction in the West and subsequently helped emerging and developing countries navigate out of financial crises and undertake investments in their development. Plans for an International Trade Organization failed, but a smaller group of countries led by the US and its European allies established the General Agreement on Tariffs and Trade (GATT) in 1948, which went on to conduct a series of successful trade negotiations culminating in the completion of the Uruguay Round in 1994. The following year, GATT evolved into the World Trade Organization, which currently establishes, revises and enforces the rules that govern international trade.

These so-called Bretton Woods institutions succeeded where the UN's institutions of international peace did not because of undisputed US and European economic dominance and leadership. With the USSR refusing to participate in them and communist China on the UN's sidelines until it took China's seat in October 1971, the two institutions were in complete alignment with Western economic philosophy of promoting more open markets. The US and Europe also dominated the decision-making through their shareholdings, with the US still holding 16.5 per cent of IMF voting rights (just above the 15 per cent required to veto decisions) and European states collectively holding over 30 per cent.[1]

Western dominance was also visible in the broader norms that were meant to guide the UN's work. The Universal Declaration of Human Rights adopted by the UN General Assembly in 1948 took as its source the European Enlightenment principles and those contained in the US Declaration of Independence, including protections against arbitrary detention (Article 9); access to an 'independent and impartial tribunal' (Article 10); 'no interference' with an individual's 'privacy ... or correspondence' (Article 12), and 'the right to freedom of opinion and expression', along with the right 'to seek, receive and impart information and ideas through any media and regardless of frontiers' (Article 19).[2]

Article 2 is clear about the universal nature of the Declaration, when it states that 'no distinction shall be made on the basis of the political, jurisdictional or international status of the country or territory to which a person belongs'. As former UN Secretary General Ban Ki-moon put it in the prologue to the 2015 illustrated edition of the Declaration, 'It has become a yardstick by which we measure right and wrong. It provides a foundation for a just and decent future for all and has given people everywhere a powerful tool in the fight against oppression, impunity and affronts to human dignity.'[3]

These principles may have been more honoured in the breach than in the observance during the last Cold War, including by US allies, but the fact that they were accepted as the guiding principles for political organization globally and as underlying requirements for the US and its allies to grant market access and economic support, underscored the hegemonic position the US held in that period.

Erosion

By 1990, it looked like the Western approach to domestic and international governance had come out on top, as Francis Fukuyama argued in his 1992 book, *The End of History and the Last Man*. Communist regimes had collapsed in much of the world, and democracies replaced autocracies from Latin America to Africa and East Asia. For a very brief period, the UN system appeared to work as its founders had intended. There was unanimous approval for military intervention in 1990 against Saddam Hussein's invasion of

Kuwait, and democratic governments seized the moment to embed their principles in two new institutions.

Following a majority vote in the UN General Assembly, the International Criminal Court (ICC) came into being in 2002 to prosecute leaders who perpetrated atrocities against their own or other citizens (although the US was among seven countries, including China, not to ratify the treaty). And in 2005, all member states of the UN endorsed the principle of 'Responsibility to Protect' (R2P), which further challenged notions of sovereignty by requiring states to take collective action if another member state proved incapable of protecting its own population against genocide, ethnic cleansing or war crimes.

But this proved to be the high-water mark of the idea of a worldwide liberal international order. Two developments, in particular, have pulled the world in a new direction, meaning that the New Cold War takes place in a very different global context.

The first is the loss of confidence throughout much of the world that a still dominant US, lacking strategic competitors, would remain a relatively benign global hegemon. Successive US administrations have always pursued their own version of US interests internationally but, as hegemons do, they did so generally within the boundaries of wanting to strengthen their alliances and draw others to America's side. The US response to the terrorist attacks of 11 September 2001 shattered this idea. The invasion of Iraq in March 2003 went ahead without full UN approval, despite it being a preventive rather than a defensive action. America's obsession with winning its 'global war on terror' led it to break several of the core tenets of the Universal Declaration. It used forced renditions to ferry suspects to locations in countries that practised torture, abused detainees at the US military base in Abu Ghraib, Iraq, and imprisoned terrorism suspects in a location, Guantanamo

Bay in Cuba, chosen specifically because it was beyond the reach of the US civil justice system.

President Obama's election was a relief to US allies, but the see-saw in US foreign policy further weakened confidence in US global leadership. Having reluctantly acceded to British and French demands to put R2P into practice and used force to prevent Libyan leader Muammar Gaddafi from massacring his opponents in 2011, the Obama administration refused to intervene in Syria, even after the Assad regime crossed his explicit 'red line' and used chemical weapons against Syrian civilians in August 2013. US voters then elected Donald Trump as president, who unilaterally withdrew the US from the Paris Agreement on climate change and moved the US embassy in Israel to East Jerusalem, despite a 2017 UN General Assembly resolution declaring the status of Jerusalem as Israel's capital 'null and void'. In his first address to the UN General Assembly in September 2017, Trump declared that 'strong, sovereign nations let diverse countries with different values, different cultures and different dreams not just co-exist but work side by side on the basis of mutual respect', terminology that was perfectly aligned with the leadership in Beijing.[4]

It is within this context that China's status as a global economic power began its transition to global political power. China is as exceptionalist in its foreign policy as any great power, as revealed by its unwillingness to condemn Moscow's invasion of Ukraine despite Chinese leaders' frequent insistence that countries should not interfere in the internal affairs of others. It has a simple vision for international order, aligned with its approach to domestic governance, which sets aside the primacy of liberal values and focuses squarely on the centrality of state sovereignty in international law and the UN system. The timing of its message could not be better. Beijing points to the chaos unleashed by America's interventions in the Middle East, and promises to focus instead on helping deliver economic development (through its Global Development Initiative), stability (through its Global Security Initiative), and mutual respect for different political systems that are rooted in distinct histories (through its Global Civilizations Initiative).[5]

Beijing has worked assiduously since 2012 to raise the profile of its vision at the UN, buying votes in the General Assembly and among non-permanent members of the Security Council by targeting financial and other support at smaller, poorer, neglected countries across Africa and the South Pacific. By 2020, it had steered Chinese nationals into leadership positions of four of the UN's fifteen agencies, although all bar one have since made way for non-Chinese successors.[6] It enjoys strong support for turning the UN's Human Rights Council from an upholder of the principles of the Universal Declaration into a check on efforts by UN officials or democratic governments to call out breaches by UN members. There are few better examples of the success of its strategy than the support China received in the Human Rights Council from Gulf states for its mass incarceration of Muslim Uighurs in Xinjiang province.[7]

And the Chinese government has made strenuous efforts in the last ten years to end the 'multi-stakeholder' approach to internet governance, favoured by the US and other democratic countries. Under this approach, scientists, company executives and representatives of civil society organizations – not governments – take the lead on writing and updating the rules for the workings of the internet and ensuring compliance. Conscious of the political as well as economic power of the internet, the Chinese and Russian governments have led the way in trying to bring its governance under the control of the International Telecommunication Union (ITU), a UN agency in which governments have the final say. Although unsuccessful to date, the Chinese approach to internet governance would legitimize the idea that governments could use mobile networks, search engines and social media platforms as a vast data reservoir for Orwellian state surveillance over their citizens.[8]

US exceptionalism makes it hard for liberal democracies to mount a fightback. Not only has the US refused to join the ICC, but it also refuses to ratify the UN Convention on the Law of the Sea, which helps adjudicate territorial disputes with China in the South China Sea, and the Comprehensive Test Ban Treaty, which is one of the pillars of the nuclear non-proliferation regime. America's allies have grown used to this US exceptionalism, not least because they benefit from its continued protection. The same cannot be said for the increasingly self-confident but frustrated countries in the Global South, who see how the US and its allies continue to protect their privileged position in the IMF and World Bank. They also justifiably see the UN Security Council, with its five veto-wielding permanent members representing a victory that they won nearly eighty years ago, as an anachronism.

Sadly, there is little prospect of modernizing the multi-lateral system in today's more competitive geopolitical context. One regular proposal, endorsed by the US and Europe as well as by China and Russia, is to increase the number of permanent members of the UN Security Council. But which mix of countries would the existing five unani-mously accept in today's divided geopolitical context, and how to pick some without offending others? Limiting the circumstances under which permanent members can use their veto was a long shot before but is near impossible now.

The same challenges face the World Bank and IMF. After a review of IMF quotas and voting weights between 2010 and 2016, China's share rose from 3.8 per cent to 6 per cent, still only a third of its share of the global economy, leaving the institution firmly under the control of the US and Europe. Following a further six-year review that concluded in December 2023, the quota shares were left unchanged. The US and its allies chose not to dilute their dominant position in the IMF or their ability to target financial support to countries with which they are aligned in the New Cold War, like Ukraine. The current voting weights also reflect the fact that China still chooses not to have a freely convertible currency and wants to keep some of the benefits of its economic status as a developing country.

Workarounds

Given the unlikely prospects of structural reform of the UN system, countries are working around it with a mix-and-match approach to global governance. New groups bring together 'like-minded' countries, clustering around the priorities and values of their main champions, the US and China, while others cut across the geopolitical divide.

On the democratic side, the main institutions are the G7, NATO, the EU, the 'Quad' (made up of Australia, India, Japan and the US) and the Paris-based Organisation for Economic Cooperation and Development (OECD). The EU is the most integrated grouping, the Quad the least. The G7 encapsulates the global interests of America and its Atlantic and Pacific allies, making it the principal coordinating body for the liberal democracies in the New Cold War. Because they share similar democratic governance systems, they can agree to rules to strengthen their collective economic security in ways that would be impossible with others. They are supported by the OECD, which brings together representatives of thirty-eight economically developed democracies to negotiate and adopt internationally respected guidelines on issues ranging from anti-corruption to fairer international corporate taxation.

On the autocratic side, Russia has created the Eurasian Economic Union (EEU), which is made up of those former members of the Soviet Union that retain close economic and political ties to Moscow. In addition to Russia, this now involves only Armenia, Belarus, Kazakhstan and Kyrgyzstan. The EEU aims to mirror the EU and remove barriers to trade and agree common standards among its members. But the Kremlin's main objective is to use it to keep as many of its closest neighbours as possible in its sphere of influence and prevent them from choosing economic partnerships with the EU instead.[9]

The country that has been most active in building new institutions over the past two decades is China. It founded the Shanghai Cooperation Organization (SCO) in 2001 to counterbalance US power and influence among its neighbours. The SCO promotes cooperation on regional security issues, including the fight against regional terrorism, ethnic separatism and religious extremism. The SCO's original members, apart from China, are India, Kazakhstan, Kyrgyzstan, Russia, Pakistan, Tajikistan and Uzbekistan. Just as the G7 is becoming a G7+ with the regular inclusion of Australia and South Korea among others to strengthen economic security within the framework of democratic values, so the SCO is expanding to include autocracies interested in strengthening their security using methods that align with their values. Reflecting this reality, in 2021 the SCO began the accession process for Iran to become a full member. The SCO has three further Observer States that are interested in acceding to full membership, Afghanistan, Belarus and Mongolia. And in 2021, Egypt, Qatar and Saudi Arabia joined six other countries (Armenia, Azerbaijan, Cambodia, Nepal, Sri Lanka and Turkey) as SCO Dialogue Partners.

China has also catalysed three institutions whose memberships cut across the new geopolitical divide. One is the

Asia Infrastructure Investment Bank (AIIB), launched in 2016 and also headquartered in Beijing, in which China is the majority shareholder. Unlike the opaque financing agreements that are part of its bilateral Belt and Road Initiative MoUs, China established the AIIB deliberately as an Asia-focused development bank that would aim to adhere to global standards of financial transparency and environmental sustainability. It is now the world's second largest development financing institution, with 106 member countries and another dozen waiting to join. The United States and Japan are the only G7 members outside the AIIB.

The other new institution is the Regional Comprehensive Economic Partnership (RCEP), which came into force in 2022. RCEP involves China for the first time inside a free trade agreement alongside its regional geopolitical rivals Japan, Australia and South Korea, as well as ASEAN members. Given its economic and political diversity, RCEP is a relatively thin trade agreement, offering only lower tariffs on trade in goods than are provided under the WTO, plus some additional regulatory transparency. But businesses operating inside RCEP benefit from favourable access to markets comprising over two billion people and representing 30 per cent of global GDP.[10]

The third and the most pertinent institution in the context of the New Cold War is the BRICS grouping, which takes its name from the acronym coined by Jim O'Neill and his Goldman Sachs research team in 2001 to highlight those countries whose growing consumer classes could make them the main new players in the global economy. As the acronym indicates, the BRICS combines China and Russia alongside Brazil, India and, since 2010, South Africa. The BRICS, which held their first summit in 2009, is now at the heart of a geo-economic initiative by Beijing and Moscow to develop an alternative

Global South club to the Global North's G7. It has momentum. Of the twenty-three countries that have applied to join the group, eighteen did so between 2022 and 2023, including the six that were invited at the BRICS summit in Johannesburg in September 2023 to join it as of January 2024 – Argentina, Egypt, Ethiopia, Iran, Saudi Arabia and the UAE. One of the BRICS members' unifying themes is their opposition to continued US dominance of the global economy, above all through its privileged position at the heart of the Bretton Woods institutions.[11]

By creating the BRICS-affiliated New Development Bank (NDB) in 2015, BRICS countries now have the chance to access development financing without the political conditionality and liberal economic requirements of the IMF and World Bank.[12] One of the NDB's priorities is to enable its Emerging Market Economy and Developing Country members to use currency swaps to settle trade between them, rather than by using the US dollar. The Chinese have also established a fledgling payments settlement system that can bypass the US and Europe-controlled SWIFT inter-bank system, and have seen the RMB's share of trade finance double to 4.5 per cent since February 2022.[13]

Rather than being a sign of strength, however, enlarging the BRICS signals China's main weakness in the New Cold War. Xi Jinping must convert China into the leader of the Global South because, if it does not lead the south, it leads no one. But, despite the lengthy list of policy topics they addressed in Johannesburg, the members of the enlarged BRICS lack a common vision other than opposition to US economic hegemony and bring instead some deep divisions, above all the strategic rivalry between China and India and, after its enlargement, between Saudi Arabia and Iran. Just as importantly, few countries in the Global South want to see a gridlocked, Western-dominated UN replaced by structural competition between the G7 on the one side and a grouping such as the BRICS led by China claiming the mantle of their new leader, on the other.

Nervousness about China's increasingly anti-US positioning of the BRICS may have contributed to Indonesia and Mexico's decision not to pursue BRICS membership in Johannesburg and the new Argentine government's withdrawal of its application. Having Russia, with its overt support for coup plotters in Africa, as well as its disdain for the sovereignty of its neighbours, as a leading force in the BRICS is another source of anxiety for some members and applicants. It is also a reminder that Russia and China's commitment to non-interference in the affairs of other countries is selective and self-serving. And the jarring disconnection between the Johannesburg summit's exhortations to promote women's leadership and the complete absence of women among China's political leadership cannot have been lost on those in attendance.

In contrast, the most inclusive workaround to the UN is the G20. Technically, the G20 stands at the apex of global economic decision-making, tasking other world bodies, like the IMF and Financial Stability Board, to develop proposals to which all countries can subscribe in order to support global economic stability. Having been expanded at the G20 summit in New Delhi in September 2023 to include the African Union (AU) as a permanent member, it now constitutes three-quarters of the world's population and nearly 90 per cent of global GDP. The G20 is also the one forum that brings the antagonists in the New Cold War together around the same table along with the world's largest non-aligned countries. Its members include all the G7+, the original five BRICS, and several other countries that are playing both sides of the new geopolitical divide, like Saudi Arabia and Turkey, or are just happy to straddle it, like Indonesia, Mexico and members of the AU.

Importantly, G20 members that are not protagonists in the New Cold War, including the last two G20 chairs

– Indonesia and India – want to use the forum to coordinate action on the global agenda, including food security and climate change, and not just on economic and financial stability. But the current geopolitical divide threatens to gridlock the G20 also. G7 members are determined to ostracize Russia for its illegal war against Ukraine. For its part, China wants to insulate the G20 from geopolitics and retain its narrow focus on global economic and financial cooperation. It was accused of blocking the development of collective positions on addressing climate change throughout the Indian G20 presidency in 2023.[14]

Xi Jinping's decision to miss the New Delhi summit implied that China considers it a bigger priority to build up the BRICS as a counterbalance to the G7 than to share the stage at the G20 with the US and other G7 members, which, with the support of some of the straddlers, might tilt decisions against it. This is what happened at the G20 summit in Bali in 2022, when the Russian and Chinese delegations were blindsided by the Indonesian presidency's decision, with India's support, to reiterate the UN General Assembly's resolution severely criticizing Russia's invasion of Ukraine in its summit declaration.

The recent experience of the G20 and the emergence of the new intergovernmental clubs and groups described above begs the question whether it and the UN, the two most inclusive multilateral institutions, can be more than just talking shops in which the powerful try to dominate the global narrative. If this is their fate, the lack of a truly global governance framework could condemn the two sides to diverge and compete in destructive ways. The prospects for addressing climate change successfully would then plummet. And the global economic opportunities that should open alongside new regional trade agreements in the Global South could be negated by the sharpening edges of the geopolitical competition in the Global North.

There may still be ways for nations to cooperate on shared global challenges, even without a global referee. But for this to happen, countries will need to find ways to live safely alongside each other in the New Cold War, by building a stable if still confrontational framework of geopolitical competition.

11

How to survive and prosper in the New Cold War

In this book I have examined ten important differences between this Cold War and the last, starting with the fact that China is on a very different trajectory to the Soviet Union. Forty years after opening up its economy, it is still marshalling its global power. It could become as economically and militarily powerful as the US, if not more so. The CCP currently has control of its destiny and is unlikely to lose it any time soon. China is not like the USSR then or Russia today in one especially important way. It is invested in globalization. It will be one of the biggest beneficiaries of continued geopolitical stability and economic openness in the twenty-first century. But unsurprisingly, given its size and history, it refuses to be a rule-taker. Instead, the CCP is attempting to rewrite the norms of today's relatively liberal international order to give primacy to state sovereignty and security above all else. As a hedge against failure or gridlock in the multilateral UN and G20, it is forming new, alternative institutions that will support its preferences for national and international governance.

Unlike the last Cold War, China now has Russia at its side. Together, they are making a concerted effort, in their words, to 'democratize' global politics, by which they mean dilute the power of the US and its allies in international institutions. The fact that the countries of the Global South are now finding their voice and have far more economic clout than in the past is a central factor in this new dynamic. It means that 'there are changes that have not happened in a hundred years', as Xi Jinping said to Putin during his visit to Moscow in March 2023. But whether China and Russia together can 'drive these changes', and mould them to their image, as Xi also told Putin when they met, is another matter altogether.[1]

With deep cultural schisms afflicting its domestic politics, the US is less internationally minded and has stepped back from geo-economic leadership. But the combination of Russia's invasion of Ukraine, China's more assertive rise and its close relationship with Russia has re-energized the transatlantic alliance and given it a far more global outlook. The alignment between Beijing and Moscow has also led to the emergence for the first time of an Atlantic–Pacific partnership, which is fusing around the G7.

It is uncertain whether the US and its allies will put most of their newfound unity and effort into resisting China and Russia, or whether they can also lift their sights to what is the biggest *global* challenge of this era – climate change. What is clear, however, is that the visions for international order on both sides are contradictory and incompatible. One will dominate the twenty-first century. If the most powerful liberal democracies still want to midwife a world in which the majority enjoy freedom of thought and expression and prize the rule of law and transparency, with governments under pressure to serve the people rather than the opposite, then they need a new playbook. Learning from our recent history and understanding the important differences between the New Cold War and the last, it is possible to identify five rules to manage this new contest. These rules can reduce the risk of devastating conflict, sustain some of the main benefits of economic globalization, revive liberal democracy, and create space for greater international cooperation on global challenges.

Rule 1: Don't create a self-fulfilling prophecy

The first rule is to do our utmost to prevent outright conflict with China from becoming a self-fulfilling prophecy; this would lead to devastating disorder for the world and not just this Cold War's protagonists.

One of the worst tendencies of governments is to interpret their opponents' intentions incorrectly and create the future that they sought to avoid. Capabilities do not always reflect intentions. And official statements today do not necessarily point to actions tomorrow. Or they might. It is easy to underestimate the danger a hostile government poses to your security, as most Europeans did when assessing Putin's intentions towards Ukraine in 2021 or indeed Hitler's in the 1930s. But we can just as easily overestimate a threat, as the George W. Bush administration did in the wake of the 9/11 attacks when it misread reports about Saddam Hussein's links to Al Qaeda and his clandestine stocks of weapons of mass destruction. The result was a failed military intervention that greatly increased Iranian influence in the heart of the Middle East.

The potential for misjudging capabilities and intentions in the New Cold War is great, and so are the implications of being wrong. It is increasingly common in the US and some parts of Europe to view China as a similar type of threat to the Soviet Union, pursuing world as well as regional domination. There is no doubt that the CCP wants to use China's growing economic and military strength to dominate its region and match the US globally. But whether these capabilities and intentions mean

China will dominate the world in the twenty-first century is questionable.

China today is riddled with internal political contradictions and economic vulnerabilities. Its biggest strength is also its biggest vulnerability. Its vast economy remains heavily dependent on external trade to sustain itself and drive growth, especially as its ageing population and resistance to immigration put a cap on future consumption. China has taken steps to try to compensate for its vulnerabilities by securing markets and resources internationally. And yet its efforts to cement these commercial relationships into political influence by enlarging the SCO and BRICS cannot hide the fact that they are groupings of expedience, which could easily shatter under stress. In contrast to the US, China remains unique among current and past great powers in having no true allies. Even China's hopes to grow its political influence in the Asia–Pacific region is hitting the buffers, largely because of its own misinterpretations of external risks and opportunities.

China misread the Obama administration's November 2011 announcement of a 'pivot to Asia', which was principally about rebuilding US relations with countries in the region. The expectation that Washington would focus on challenging militarily China's claims in the South China Sea led Beijing to seize reefs and islands there between 2013 and 2015, and to break its promise not to install military facilities on them. The result has been a Pyrrhic victory in terms of China's regional influence.

In March 2018, communist Vietnam welcomed the first in a series of port visits by a US aircraft carrier. In September 2021, Australia signed the AUKUS partnership with the US and the UK that will give it nuclear-powered submarines capable of ranging across the Pacific. That same year witnessed a significant increase in freedom of navigation operations through the South China Sea by the US and its allies. In February 2023, the Philippines designated four new bases adjacent to China to host rotating US forces under their bilateral Enhanced Defense Cooperation Agreement, strengthening America's defensive 'first island chain'. And in August 2023, Japan, South Korea and the US signed their historic trilateral partnership at Camp David.

Much as Putin misjudged NATO members' reactions to his invasion of Ukraine and gave the alliance a newfound purpose and strength, so Xi's handling of America's pivot to Asia has helped Washington strengthen its relations with its Pacific allies and neighbours.

How might misperceptions and mistakes affect the main potential flashpoint of the New Cold War: Taiwan? President Xi has made clear that China aims to reunify Taiwan with the mainland by 2049, at the latest. Official statements still emphasize 'peaceful unification', but Xi has refused to rule out the use of force.[2] The massive build-up in China's military capabilities around Taiwan over the past decade, and recent exercises for amphibious landings, have triggered the succession of statements by senior US commanders saying they believe conflict between the US and China is inevitable and imminent – maybe as early as 2025.

But do Chinese capabilities and exercises around Taiwan equal intentions? China's leadership could just as easily be putting its forces into a position where, should a future Taiwanese government cross Beijing's reddest line by declaring independence, they would not be deterred by US military superiority from blockading the island into reversing course. Rather than a highly risky and costly invasion, Beijing's preferred method for reuniting with Taiwan could still be the 'anaconda strategy' – trying to constrict Taiwan economically, politically and diplomatically into unification by 2049.[3]

These two diametrically different scenarios raise the risk that one side's misinterpretation leads to the other's mistaken action. For example, an increase in the quality and quantity of US weapons sales to Taiwan to help it deter a Chinese attack could lead the Chinese leadership to conclude that they should attack before a future Taiwanese leader has the deterrent capability to declare independence.

Given the deep concerns in Washington and allied capitals over China's future capabilities and intentions, there are many who believe the threat warrants the move to a formal policy of containment, just as the US sought to contain the Soviet Union for much of the last Cold War. This would entail going beyond trade and investment restrictions and efforts to strengthen America's political-military relations with Asia–Pacific countries. Containment would mean trying to use trade restrictions to prevent China's economy from prospering, so it could not become stronger militarily, while exacerbating China's internal weaknesses. It implies using external pressure to try to drive a wedge between the CCP and the Chinese people that would lead to some form of regime change.[4]

There are several drawbacks to this approach. For the time being at least, China is a better governed country than the USSR ever was. Over the last three decades, despite its deep insecurities and the daunting task ahead, the CCP has delivered major improvements in the welfare of most of China's population, and there is no meaningful or sizeable domestic opposition to its rule. Pursuing a policy of containment, with its subtext of favouring political destabilization, would fuel the party's insecurity. The CCP would most likely respond by inflaming Chinese popular nationalism, leading to dangerous potential spillovers, including over the status of Taiwan. China's leaders would also cleave even closer to Moscow and to other countries with little interest in promoting international stability, like North Korea and Iran, which would run counter to American and allied interests. And it is highly unlikely that the world would be a safer place if a country of China's size imploded under external pressure.

For now, given the uncertainties over China's future capabilities and intentions, the logic of containment does not outweigh the alternative, which is to continue resisting China's actions that undermine regional stability and good global governance, while engaging judiciously with China economically and on tackling global challenges, leaving the CCP and the Chinese people to deal as best they can with their internal contradictions. Only a change in the thinking of the Chinese leadership, with or without popular pressure, is likely to change the country politically for the better in a sustainable way. If China suffers an economic catastrophe or even a civil war, it would be best that other countries had no hand in precipitating it.

But following the rule of strategic patience and biding one's time, as Deng Xiaoping put it, requires the US and its democratic allies to do so from a position of strength. An increasingly authoritarian and assertive China with world-class military and technological capabilities poses serious threats to its neighbours and to the international order to which liberal democracies aspire.

Rule 2: Rally the liberal democracies

As the number of functioning democracies across the world declines, and some flirt with authoritarianism, democratic leaders need to prove once again that they offer the most effective model of governance for dealing with the challenges of the twenty-first century. On most measures and in most domains, the US and its allies still stand at the top of the world league tables (if you exclude those small countries with exceptional wealth from natural resources). This is easy to forget, when the middle classes in America and many of its allies are struggling with the impacts of globalization and technological innovation, putting their social contracts under severe stress. Although the path is very difficult politically for each country, the keys to their rejuvenation at least lie in their hands, whether this involves upgrading their physical and digital infrastructure, delivering more sustainable energy, or reforming their education, health, pension and social care systems. One of their biggest new challenges is to manage the politics of apportioning and integrating the growing but much needed influx of young immigrants from the conflict-ridden and poorest countries in the Global South.

Given the scale of these challenges, the ability of democracies to build a path to more sustainable and equitable growth will also benefit from teamwork – pooling their resources and investing together in their economic security and strategic resilience. The current G7, which includes the EU, is the logical forum to do this, but enlarging the G7 into a G9 by including South Korea and Australia would be a powerful signal that the major liberal democracies allied to the US and threatened by the China–Russia alignment will consistently coordinate policies to enhance their technological strength and collective economic security.

With South Korea and Australia formally in the mix, the G9 could avoid repeating Europe's mistake of over-reliance on Russia for its energy security in the late carbon era by relying on China for their renewable energy in the early green era. Instead, together with other partners, they can coordinate a reduction in their dependence on China for critical green technologies and imports, such as EV batteries and processed rare earths. They can also strengthen their supply chains for new telecommunications technologies and semiconductors for AI and quantum computing.

South Korea is one of the world's leading developers of 6G communications and producers of advanced semiconductors and batteries, while Australia is the world's largest producer of lithium and fourth largest of uranium (G7 member Canada is second). Whereas Australia's commodities fed China's rise as an industrial power, Australia is in a position now to feed the rise of the G9 community as a global power in green energy.

Today, the G9 countries account for 50 per cent of world GDP and over 60 per cent of global defence spending, with only 14 per cent of world population.[5] As importantly, they also constitute roughly 65 per cent of spending on research and development by the top twelve R&D spenders[6] and for twenty-two of the world's top twenty-five universities,[7] and, together, they challenge China's dominance of annual patent filings. The total number of patents filed by the US, Japan, South Korea and the EU stood at 1.3 million to China's 1.6 million in 2021.[8]

But the G9's aggregate capabilities are not just a list of statistics, as they are for members of the SCO or the enlarged BRICS. This club of liberal democracies can develop high technology and critical supply chains collectively because their interdependence is built upon the strategic trust that comes from sharing a common set of values and governance systems, as well as a deepening and interlacing set of security alliances and partnerships. This is in stark contrast to the BRICS, where India has banned many Chinese technology companies from operating in its market because of security concerns; or where Saudi Arabia and Iran could fall out at any moment over regional security.

To be more effective in the future, the G9 grouping would benefit from a small, intergovernmental secretariat to ensure policy continuity and delivery. It could help monitor agreed joint investments and prepare contingency plans for coordinating sanctions and other economic responses should there be an escalation in tensions with China, Russia or another member of the autocratic club.

There also needs to be a serious focus on defence and deterrence if the world's leading liberal democracies are to follow the path of strategic patience towards China and be prepared to deter Russia and other autocratic governments that seek to challenge them. The more autocracies there are in the world, the more likely they are to externalize their internal insecurities. Credible deterrence against external coercion will be a central pillar of the G9's independence of action in the New Cold War, just as it was for the West in the last. Strengthening collective security will depend on closer consultation and coordination between NATO and America's Pacific alliances. It will also depend on consistent financial investment by all G9 countries, not just the US, in modern, deployable forces, state-of-the-art communications, asymmetric civil–military innovation, counter-disinformation, technological interoperability and regular training.

There will undoubtedly be hiccups and rifts between the G9 on levels of defence spending, as there will be on technical standards for AI development or the privacy requirements for data sharing. Europeans will continue to be more risk-averse towards technological innovation than their US counterparts, prioritizing the 'precautionary principle' to limit the speed of rolling out new AI, for example, or the development of new internet applications. They and their Pacific counterparts might resist US efforts to expand restrictions on investments in and from China. But the reality of closer Chinese and Russian alignment has already spurred an impressive level of harmonization between the US and its allies on defensive economic measures towards China, in addition to sanctions on Russia. And current European investment in more practical and less rhetorical commitments to security in the Indo-Pacific means they are no longer passive observers of their Asian allies' security interests. With greater confidence in their collective economic resilience and military capabilities, the US and its allies will be better placed to pursue consistent policies towards China and minimize the risk of misunderstandings and mistakes.

At the same time, building up the G9 as quickly as possible is essential given the uncertainties around America's future willingness to play a global leadership role, especially on international economic policy, whoever has the keys to the White House. The sooner the G9 can establish the structures and habits of deeper cooperation, the better placed the liberal democratic camp will be to manage and, hopefully, weather any disruption, especially should Trump or a similar-minded person come to power in 2025 or beyond.[9]

Rule 3: Build a framework for peaceful economic competition

The idea that we should avoid growing levels of trade and investment with China in the New Cold War contains its own set of risks. It would cut across the integrated supply chains and open trading arrangements that have improved the livelihoods of citizens inside the G9 and across the world. It would test the cohesion of the G9 countries, whose unity is so important, but whose economic exposure to the Chinese market differs widely. It would contribute to price volatility and sharpen inflationary pressures within the G9 and globally. In contrast, trade and investment between G9 countries and China in non-critical economic sectors, such as cars and car parts, consumer electronics, civilian purpose machine tools, luxury goods, clothing, processed foods, financial and other services and entertainment can be in both sides' interest, even if dependence on imports of sensitive items like semiconductors, telecoms equipment or processed rare earths will not.

Using greater restrictions on trade and investment as a geo-economic tool to try to weaken China may also fail. China has surrounded itself with economic partners and political followers across the world, which would blunt the potential effects of economic containment. Moreover, ratcheting up unnecessarily the limits on G9 trade and investment with China would empower Russia by cementing its relationship with China.

Providing G9 countries are successful in reducing their critical dependencies on Chinese suppliers, and providing they are ready to push back against unfair Chinese competition, then it would be better to continue to grow the economic relationship across the roughly 90 per cent of activity that has no security implications. It would also be better for G9 countries to remain engaged in the future success of the Chinese economy, rather than let the opportunities for political leverage that this engagement brings decline alongside lower levels of trade and investment. There is no reason why a relatively open trading relationship should not go hand in hand with a willingness to contest China's breaches of international law in the South China Sea or its efforts to rewrite rules at the UN. A lack of critical dependencies on China and a coherent G9 would help its members in future resist the sort of economic coercion many of them have suffered from China in the past.

This is the logic behind efforts in G9 capitals to focus on designing protections that would avoid widespread economic decoupling from China. For example, the Biden administration advocates building what it describes as a 'small yard with a high fence' for its high technology relationship with China.[10] The approach involves identifying specific technologies on which the US restricts exports and investment to and from China to avoid the perverse outcome of helping it become a more formidable military and strategic competitor.

Delineating what is and is not critical can be difficult. Some argue, for example, that it is sufficient for the US to keep one or two generations ahead of China on key technologies. But Jake Sullivan, the US National Security Advisor, has said the US will now pursue the more open-ended goal of maintaining 'as large of a lead as possible'.[11] The risk is that the US will keep enlarging the yard, as it concludes that other sectors are critical to its strategic competition with China. For example, advances in bioengineering could be used to build new bioweapons or even enhance human cognitive and physical capabilities so as to create 'super soldiers'. Chinese companies might have to be denied access to US-based cloud computing services, given that their size and computing power could allow China to train its AI systems without importing restricted US graphics processing units.[12] Some members of the US Congress want to restrict imports of Chinese EV batteries and processed rare earth metals in case these allow China to hold a seemingly non-critical sector like car manufacturing hostage in the event of a serious deterioration of bilateral relations or the outbreak of a military conflict.[13] Others consider US financial services exports to China to be critical, as they would help the CCP manage the risks posed by China's ageing population.

But these uncertainties do not take away from the fact that the Biden administration's approach is solid. It supports trade, while targeting export and investment restrictions on any technology that would directly strengthen China or another rival as a military competitor. And it seeks to construct common approaches among the G9 countries in their economic relations with China and other rivals so as to strengthen the group's coherence and value in the New Cold War. In fact, the diversity of G9 interests and experience can help them triage the critical from non-critical technologies and sectors and thereby design the most viable guard rails possible.

Chinese leaders reject the entire approach of 'derisking' G9 countries' trade with China, believing it is designed purely to hold them back economically. Chinese Vice President Han Zheng declared at a conference I attended at Tsinghua University in Beijing in July 2023 that 'derisking is the biggest risk'. But, as Xi's Made in China 2025 strategy clearly implied, China always intended to develop its own high-technology capabilities as quickly as possible and by whatever means, including subsidized domestic innovation, forced intellectual property transfer and industrial espionage. The sensible approach for the G9 is to make China work harder for longer to try to catch up, and to try to keep it one step behind in certain important technologies.

Rule 4: Don't neglect arms control

While the US and its allies are giving serious thought to building a framework for peaceful economic competition with China, one crucial area where there is no such framework, and where there will need to be if we are to manage the New Cold War successfully, is arms control.

Despite agreeing in November 2023 to resume high-level military contacts, Chinese leaders believe that entering into formal negotiations with the US to reduce the risk of a confrontation in the South China Sea would call into question their sovereign claims in the region. As Cui Tiankai, former Chinese Ambassador to the US, said at the same conference I attended in July 2023, 'we are not interested in guard rails on the wrong path'. In contrast, they believe that the lack of agreed rules of engagement between Chinese and its rivals' naval and air forces operating around disputed maritime areas can serve as a deterrent to US forces. Nevertheless, US leaders correctly persist in trying to convince their Chinese counterparts to establish a reliable 'hot line' between their military commands to help avoid or defuse future incidents.

The situation concerning nuclear weapons is equally perilous. A dangerous nuclear arms race is now under way, which has reawakened the spectres of an accidental launch and of nuclear weapons proliferation. In 2019, the Trump administration pulled the US out of the 1987 Intermediate-Range Nuclear Forces (INF) Treaty with Russia, which banned the production as well as the deployment of ballistic or cruise missiles with a range between 500 and 5,500 kilometres, whether they carried conventional or nuclear warheads. This was partly because US security officials were convinced that Russia had been secretly and illegally modernizing its missiles under this category since at least 2015. But they were also concerned that China's absence from the INF Treaty was allowing it to develop missiles within this range that could put the US at a disadvantage in the Pacific theatre if it remained constrained by its agreement with Russia.

Beijing's current priority is not arms control. It wants to build a stockpile of warheads and launch vehicles that will put it on a par with the United States and Russia this decade. In June 2020, it refused an invitation to join the US and Russia in discussions to extend the 2011 New Strategic Arms Reduction Treaty (START), the last remaining strategic nuclear arms control treaty between the US and Russia, which imposes limits on the total number of strategic (intercontinental) warheads and launchers each side can possess and provides a framework for regular verification inspections.

In August 2022, following the outbreak of the Ukraine war and the firm US response, Vladimir Putin announced that Russia was suspending US inspections of its nuclear forces under START. And, in January 2023, the Biden administration stated that Russia was no longer in compliance with the treaty's obligations, meaning it could lapse when it is due to expire in February 2026. Senior US policymakers now fear the US could face a joint Russia–China nuclear threat that would be twice the size of its own arsenal, requiring the US to build up its capabilities significantly.[14] So long as the idea of bilateral and trilateral nuclear arms control negotiations between the US, China and Russia remains stalemated, the risks of a nuclear confrontation – accidental or deliberate – will grow.

The emergence of the New Cold War also makes the commitments that the recognized nuclear armed states made under the 1968 Nuclear Non-Proliferation Treaty to do away with all nuclear weapons at some point in the future even more fanciful. This could, in turn, convince one or more of the non-nuclear states to acquire similar means of strategic defence or coercion against their rivals, breaking the dam for others.

Brazil, Argentina, Iran, Japan, South Korea, Saudi Arabia and Turkey all have or could gain access to the technical capacity to develop nuclear weapons as well as their delivery systems. Those that are US allies are understandably concerned about the long-term credibility of the US extended deterrent, should China or Iran or Russia make an aggressive move against them that did not directly threaten the US or its forces.[15] And all of them have witnessed Russia successfully use threats of nuclear escalation to dissuade NATO and the US from providing as much military support to Ukraine as they might otherwise have done.

The drift towards nuclear weapons proliferation may already be unstoppable. But the United States must persist in putting the issue of nuclear weapons on to its agenda with China, to test its openness to improved transparency on nuclear doctrine and capabilities and with an eye to establishing some confidence-building measures in the future. Ideally, these discussions would not be limited to numbers of nuclear warheads and missile delivery systems, but also include possible rules to protect nuclear command and control systems, whether from attack in space, through cyber warfare or, as intimated at the Biden–Xi summit in San Francisco on 15 November 2023, by misuse of AI.

Timely US–China discussions over nuclear forces and doctrine could establish frameworks and build confidence for parallel discussions on conventional arms control in the Indo-Pacific, before the ongoing arms build-up by all the regional powers and their allies makes this even harder.

Rule 5: Partner with the Global South on sustainable development

The fifth rule is that we should put as much effort into working with countries in the Global South on their priorities as we are into prevailing against China and Russia in the New Cold War. Stemming the process of climate change and transitioning to models of more sustainable and inclusive economic development are objectives on which the liberal democracies can make a meaningful difference; they are objectives on which our credibility will be rightly judged and from whose success we will also benefit. Liberal democracies cannot prevail without the support of the Global South; the battle for the Global South is the battle for control of the twenty-first century.

If we want countries from the Global South to be our partners in building a better future, and if we want to avoid them being drawn further into the orbit of Chinese influence or succumbing to Russia's efforts to sow discord, then we must not let the New Cold War be an impediment to cooperating with them on their climate and development challenges. The question is how and, above all, *how to do so now*, when the UN system and structures of multilateral cooperation are largely gridlocked. There are several options for the liberal democracies.

Above all, we should treat the large and diverse set of countries in the Global South as partners to progress. Given their growing economies, Indian decisions between investing in new coal plants or more solar power, Brazilian decisions on how to develop their agriculture and exploit their tropical resources, African approaches to mining, protection of biodiversity, and low-carbon urbanization will all help determine whether the world meets the Sustainable Development Goals. Global South countries can be pioneers on sustainable development, whether through Argentinian techniques of 'dry tilling' to promote low-carbon farming, or innovations in the development of sustainable biofuels in Kenya, Tanzania and other African countries. India's recent successes in lunar exploration open a vista to joint research with established space powers on the feasibility of mining for minerals on the moon, or further afield in our solar system. With the right technical support, African countries could undertake the genetic sequencing of new viruses locally, becoming key links in the early warning chain for global health.

For these reasons, we need to build two-way bridges to the countries in the Global South and to the regional trade groupings they are developing. In the absence of a major multilateral trade agenda, and with the US holding back from pursuing new trade agreements, the EU, Australia, Canada, Japan and the UK need to agree or complete agreements with the African Continental Free Trade Area, with Mercosur and ASEAN, helping these groupings lift the ambition of their market-opening goals in the process.

Better access to our wealthy consumer markets will be an important prize for countries in the Global South, just as access to the latter's growing populations and burgeoning middle classes will be a valuable counteroffer. As discussed in Chapter 6, many businesses have become jaded trying to penetrate the Chinese domestic market profitably and some fear that exposure to the Chinese market could be a serious risk in the event of a crisis over Taiwan. They are looking to markets across the Global South as important alternatives.

There are strategic as well as economic reasons for doing this. Unless markets and businesses in poorer parts of the Global South become more successful, their growing populations will migrate north in ever growing numbers, undermining the internal and collective political cohesion of the liberal democracies. At the same time, political elites in the Global South will become more enmeshed in opaque deals with China and Russia. Offering them alternative options matters if liberal democracies are to prevail in the New Cold War. Japan set an important example of this strategic approach to trade policy when it led the formation of the Comprehensive and Progressive Agreement for Trans-Pacific Partnership after the Trump administration pulled out of what had been a top priority of the Obama administration in its effort to counterbalance China's growing regional economic clout.

One worry is that the EU's decision to introduce carbon tariffs on imports will stunt developing countries' nascent manufacturing industries by negating the cheaper labour costs of their exports with a tariff on their carbon content. Instead, the EU needs to create incentives for developing countries to add economic value to their natural resources at home and move up the value chain, if necessary by offering them targeted carve-outs from the carbon tariff, as they do with other tariffs. There has been long-standing criticism of Chinese companies' practice of creating little local employment in Africa and of striking opaque deals that mainly extract resources, often at high environmental cost, rather than building local manufacturing. European governments and companies must make a better offer.

This applies especially to infrastructure investment. The US and its allies caught on late to the impact of China's large infrastructure projects across Africa, Latin America and Asia.[16] Despite saddling some of its recipients with unsustainable debt, investment by Chinese companies to African countries alone totalling over $600 billion between 2006 and 2021 has had a transformative impact. The launch of the Partnership for Global Infrastructure and Investment (PGI) at the G7 summit in Germany in 2022 was a long overdue but important response. It is designed to coordinate the deployment of up to $600 billion globally by 2027 in support of projects to deliver green energy, better transportation links, supply chain resilience, and digital infrastructure.

Encouragingly, the US and other G7 leaders then teamed up with India, Saudi Arabia and the UAE at the G20 summit in New Delhi the following year to announce plans to create a new India–Middle East–Europe Economic Corridor, building ports, rail, clean energy and digital infrastructure that will connect India, via the Gulf states, through Jordan and Israel, and across the Mediterranean to Europe. The US and EU also announced an initiative to build transport and clean energy infrastructure linking the Democratic Republic of the Congo and Zambia to the port of Lobito in Angola, to help develop the trade in critical minerals.[17]

Although these initiatives lack the centralized impetus of China's BRI, the intermixing of financing from the US Development Finance Corporation and the EU's Global Gateway will ensure that PGI projects operate to shared standards of good governance in terms of anti-corruption, environmental sustainability and female inclusion. The risk, of course, is that these requirements delay the speed at which project plans become reality. But, given the strategic and economic urgency, these investments could be transformational.

While physical infrastructure will be critical to the future of the Global South, digital infrastructure will be the backbone of modern, less-carbon-intensive economic development. The PGI has rightly targeted this sector for investment. But another area where the US and its allies need to engage more actively with the Global South is over approaches to domestic governance of the internet. Chinese companies' investments in a 'Digital Silk Road' around the Global South offer well-priced, high-technology opportunities for local economic modernization. But these technologies will be counterproductive if they can also be used to entrench authoritarian and, in many cases, failing governments by imposing digital state surveillance that limits freedom of expression and sharing information online.

So far, the champions of an open internet retain the upper hand. Governments that want to insert a more intrusive role for the state in internet governance must copy China and build elaborate national firewalls that prevent citizens from accessing foreign internet sites. This splintering of the internet and the data that courses through it may allow them to maintain their surveillance systems, but at a cost to their citizens' connectivity and potentially to their businesses' competitiveness and innovation.

Not all G9 country initiatives to support sustainable development in the Global South need to be undertaken against or without China. Cooperation with China on global infrastructure can sometimes help the world make progress towards its sustainable development goals. Since its foundation, the China-led Asia Infrastructure Investment Bank has co-financed sixty projects with the US-led World Bank.[18] And, whereas currencies have become an area of growing geo-economic competition in the New Cold War, the AIIB proposed in June 2023 to use its capital surplus to issue $1 billion in guarantees against sovereign-backed loans made by the World Bank.[19] This will enable the World Bank to provide new lending, while the AIIB can increase its lending to low-income borrowers.

Joint research and investment with China on carbon extraction, carbon capture and utilization, and other green technologies could provide valuable breakthroughs at scale to tackle climate change. And such cooperation need not constitute a security risk, as it does on extreme ultraviolet lithography to manufacture advanced semi-conductors, for example. Under the Biden administration, combating climate change and improving planetary health has been viewed as a way of building bridges with China. Still, unless the US engages with China in the practical process of developing green solutions together, Beijing will continue to see its comments about cooperation on combating climate change simply as a diplomatic lever to try to defuse geopolitical tensions.

China's ambivalence towards multilateral organizations that it cannot control offers one more avenue to deepen liberal democracies' relations productively with countries in the Global South. Chinese refusal to engage in the Indian government's plans for its G20 presidency in 2023 creates a new opportunity to reach out to some of those countries that generally resent US dominance and its sometimes high-handed promotion of democratic forms of governance.

To do so, G9 countries should seek to elevate the G20 as the premier forum for agreeing progress on global governance. This means not trying to use it as a forum to score geopolitical points against China or Russia, as the US and Europeans initially did over Ukraine during India's G20 presidency. Instead, it will involve supporting the more expansive global agenda favoured by countries like Brazil, Mexico, India and Indonesia. This agenda reaches beyond topics dealing specifically with economic and financial stability to include climate change and food security. Approaches to the governance of artificial intelligence and the types of capabilities to which it can safely be used would be an additional topic that fits this remit.

Importantly, all these topics lend themselves to the multi-stakeholder approach to problem solving that democratic governments support and that the G20 process has embraced. One of the biggest differences between the two sides of the New Cold War lies in their view of the role of civil society organizations, whether these are climate NGOs, labour unions, business associations, women's leadership groups, private philanthropies or think tanks. Unlike China and Russia, which ban or control these groups, the G20 process seeks their input through its work streams for the T20 (convening think tanks), the L20 (for labour unions), N20 (for NGOs), and W20 (for women's inclusion and empowerment), which run in parallel and feed their ideas into the G20's governmental working groups. While the impact of their ideas depends on the character and openness of the chairing government, they can at least put new ideas on the table and serve as a counterweight to what otherwise might be lowest-common-denominator conclusions.

With the UN's multilateral institutions creaking under the hostile stand-off of the New Cold War, representatives of civil society and business are now joining 'sub-state' national leaders – such as mayors and state governors – to work with national governments on designing and implementing responses to global policy priorities. The

G20 matters all the more, therefore, not only because it is inclusive geographically, but also because it challenges the autocratic model by exposing more countries to the benefits of political inclusion and pluralism.

Conclusion

The New Cold War is now well and truly under way. It is a Cold War because the US and China both believe the other represents a fundamental danger to their security if not their survival. The division between them is, at its roots, ideological; it pits those in China who believe in the supremacy of one-party, autocratic political systems and are willing to go to extreme lengths to protect it, against a United States whose leaders, with a few exceptions, believe that liberal democratic governance, despite all its faults, is the only way to deliver sustainable economic development at home and peace for the world. The division is also geopolitical: the CCP leadership in Beijing has correctly concluded that the US wants to block China's ability to catch up technologically in order to hold it back from becoming the dominant power in the Asia–Pacific and America's global equal.

In this sense, the stand-off between the US and China carries worrying echoes of 1938–40, when Japan's leaders saw that the US was ready to take advantage of their island country's economic dependence on oil imports to hold back its ambition to become the dominant power in the Asia–Pacific. The reaction in Beijing, for now, is not to see US technological containment as a *casus belli*; it is to reduce China's dependence on the US and its allies and to keep expanding its network of friends. But we are only at the beginning of the security dilemma between China and the

US, which continues to intensify their mutual suspicion and their geopolitical and geo-economic competition.

There are echoes also of 1914, when unprecedentedly high levels of global trade failed to prevent a rising imperial Germany and increasingly overstretched British Empire from sleepwalking into a devastating conflict. And there are parallels to the first decade of the last Cold War, leading up to the Cuban Missile Crisis, when there were no arms control agreements between the US and the Soviet Union, nor hotlines to help defuse the crisis. In that case, the two sides drew back from the brink at the last moment, but it was a close-run affair. It is impossible to know whether the contest over the future of Taiwan will be like that over the Balkans in 1914, whose fate ended up triggering the First World War, or Cuba in 1962, which helped the US and Soviet Union find a new way of living side by side, even if under the shadow of mutually assured destruction.

The same questions arise today, therefore, as at the dawn of the first Cold War and other pivotal shifts in global power: can we avoid a hot war, and which group of countries and which political system will dominate the century? The answers lie to a large extent in understanding the differences between this Cold War and the last. As this book explains, some are a deep source of concern: above all, the US is no longer comfortable playing the role of a global economic leader, while China is building a new axis of authoritarian states to maximize its global influence and to compensate for its sense of regional insecurity.

But other differences offer important notes of optimism. The deepening interconnections between the transatlantic and transpacific wings of America's global alliances suggest that the liberal democracies can prevail again in the New Cold War. Meanwhile, the United States and China are economically interdependent in ways that the US and the Soviet Union never were during their global contest. This means the US and China are having to reverse into the New Cold War, which creates pressures to avoid conflict and constituencies for compromise on both sides. What former Australian Prime Minister Kevin Rudd describes as 'managed strategic competition' should be possible rather than an inevitable descent into a hot war.[1]

Another positive difference is that this Cold War is far less binary than the last. China, Russia and the US and its allies no longer dominate the global landscape. They share it with countries in the Global South whose demographic and economic heft gives them added influence and agency. The fact that the two sides are being forced to seek the support of the Global South and take its concerns seriously means that there is less chance of the world sinking into a bipolar stand-off. There is pressure on the two main protagonists to attenuate the intensity of their competition and find avenues for cooperation on shared global challenges.

Who wins the twenty-first century will depend on who can appeal most successfully to the Global South. Xi seems to have understood this earlier than his democratic counterparts, driving new levels of investment and deepening diplomatic linkages across Latin America, Asia and Africa. But by trying to fold China's strategy to lead the Global South into enlarging the BRICS, he has made a serious mistake. The group is structurally flawed by the profound diversity of political outlooks and foreign policy priorities among its members and their lack of shared values. In contrast, the G9 are united by their values and by explicit commitments to support each other's security, even if their interests and instincts sometimes diverge. Their collective strengths should be more than a match for the BRICS grouping. Working closely together, the G9 have the markets, technology, and financial and business expertise to help countries in the Global South move up the economic value chain. And, providing they engage with these countries as more equal partners, this support will help rekindle the attractiveness of the open, democratic model for their governments, citizens and businesses alike.

This optimistic future for the world remains hostage to one critical unknown: the trajectory of US domestic politics. The presidential election in November 2024 will reveal once again how deeply divided Americans are about the essence of their national identity and their country's role in the world. Depending on the choice they make, it is possible that the US will return to a more insular outlook that downgrades the importance of alliances and allies, rescinds US commitments to combat climate change and puts America's own narrow interests as the lodestar for its foreign policy. In the lead-up to the presidential primaries, Donald Trump promised 'retribution' should he be selected as the Republican candidate and then retake the White House in 2025.[2]

But the risks of another Trump or Trumpian presidency simply make it even more important that America's European and Pacific allies strengthen their bonds now and set a path of closer engagement with the Global South. We must be ready to pick up the baton as champions of liberal democracy globally if the United States sets it to one side, and hope that it will not be for long.

Notes

Introduction

1. Gazette Staff, 'Balloon spotted over Billings being investigated as Chinese spying airship', *Billings Gazette*, 4 February 2023.
2. Chen Qingqing, Liu Xuanzun, 'China expresses dissatisfaction and protest over US shooting down civilian airship; US sets bad precedent', *Global Times*, 5 February 2023.
3. Nancy A. Youssef, 'Chinese Balloon used US Tech to Spy on Americans', *Wall Street Journal*, 29 June 2023; Phil Stewart, Mike Stone, 'US military comes to grips with over-reliance on Chinese imports', Reuters, 2 October 2018.
4. Robert Jervis, 'Cooperation under the Security Dilemma', *World Politics* 30 (January 1978), 167–214. The concept of the security dilemma was originated by John Herz, *Political Realism and Political Idealism* (University of Chicago Press, 1951).
5. 'U.S. four-star general warns of war with China in 2025', Reuters, 28 January 2023; Jesse Johnson, 'Former U.S. Indo-Pacific Commander underscores threat to Taiwan's outlying islands', *Japan Times*, 25 January 2023.
6. Graham Allison, 'Thucydides's trap has been sprung in the Pacific', *Financial Times*, 21 August 2012; and *Destined for War: Can the United States and China Escape the Thucydides Trap?* (Houghton Mifflin Harcourt, 2017).
7. In an interview with Niall Ferguson at the Bloomberg New Economy Forum in 2019, Henry Kissinger famously said that, 'we are still in the foothills of a cold war', *Bloomberg News*, 21 November 2019. Ferguson and former US Secretary of State Condoleezza Rice discuss the differences they see between the US–Soviet and US–China rivalry in 'The World Ahead: The United States in 2024', *The Economist*, 13 November 2023. For a history of the serial dawnings of a 'new Cold War' after 1990, see Gilbert Achcar, *The New Cold War: The US, China and Russia from Kosovo to Ukraine* (Saqi Books, 2023).

8. 'Joint Statement of the Russian Federation and the People's Republic of China on the International Relations Entering a New Era and the Global Sustainable Development', *Russian Ministry of Foreign Affairs*, 4 February 2022.
9. 'For AUKUS Agreement: Devil is in the Details', *National Defense Magazine*, 14 March 2023.
10. 'Full text of Xi Jinping's speech at first session of the 14th NPC', *Xinhua*, 14 March 2023; Eryk Bagshaw, 'Xi urges officials to "fight", accuses US of "encircling" China', *Sydney Morning Herald*, 7 March 2023.

1: China is no Soviet Union

1. Zbigniew Brzezinski, *Game Plan: A Geostrategic Framework for the Conduct of the U.S.–Soviet Contest* (Atlantic Monthly Press, 1986).
2. Angus Maddison, *The World Economy* (OECD, 2006), p. 185.
3. The Soviet Union accounted for c. 10 per cent of world GDP in 1990; Russia accounted for c. 3 per cent in 2021. See Nicolas Veron, 'Putin's Russia may echo the Soviet bloc, but it is far smaller', *PIIE*, 7 April 2022.
4. 'GDP per capita 1960–23', *Macrotrends* (data source, World Bank).
5. China Power Project, 'Is China Succeeding at Eradicating Poverty?' *Center for Strategic and International Studies*.
6. Katharina Buchholz, 'Which countries' students are getting most involved in STEM?', *World Economic Forum*, 20 March 2023.
7. Daitian Li, Tony W. Tong, Yangao Xiao, 'Is China Emerging as the Global Leader in AI?', *Harvard Business Review*, 18 February 2021.
8. 'China's Population is Shrinking', *The Economist*, 17 January 2023.
9. Yihan Ma, 'Percentage of savings among young people in China', *Statista*, 26 August 2022.
10. Mandy Zuo, 'Lying Flat is no more', *South China Morning Post*, 4 October 2022.
11. 'Full text of Xi Jinping's speech at the first session of the 14th NPC', 13 March 2023.
12. Zheng Wang, *Never Forget National Humiliation: Historical Memory in Chinese Politics and Foreign Relations* (Columbia University Press, 2012).
13. Xi Jinping, ibid.
14. Office of the Secretary of Defense, *Military and Security Developments Involving the People's Republic of China 2023*, US Department of Defense, p. VIII.

15. Demetri Sevastopulo, Kathrin Hille, 'China tests new space capability with hypersonic missile', *Financial Times*, 16 October 2021.
16. Fei Su, Xiao Liang, 'Ten-Year Review of China's Defense Budget: Steadily towards Modernization', *South Asian Voices, Stimson Center*, 8 June 2023.
17. China Power Project, 'How is China's Energy Footprint Changing?', *Center for Strategic and International Studies*.
18. James McBride, Noah Berman, Noah Chatzky, 'China's massive Belt and Road Initiative', *Council on Foreign Relations*, 2 February 2023.
19. Adam Gallagher, Sarhang Hamasaeed, Garrett Nada, 'What you Need to Know about China's Saudi–Iran Deal', *United States Institute of Peace*, 16 March 2023.
20. Vincent Brussee, 'China's Social Credit Score: Untangling Myth from Reality', *MERICS*, 11 February 2022.
21. Lee Jones, Shahar Ameriri, 'Debunking the Myth of Debt Trap Diplomacy', *Chatham House Research Paper*, August 2020; '"Jewel in the Crown": The Troubles of Kenya's China-Funded Train', *New York Times*, 7 August 2022.

2: Reversing into the New Cold War

1. 'GDP (current US$)', *The World Bank* (https://data.worldbank.org).
2. This comparison uses 2020 US dollars. James N. Miller, Michael O'Hanlon, 'Focusing on quality over quantity in the US military budget', *Brookings Institution Report*, 2 December 2019.
3. 'The immigrant population in the US is increasing again', NPR, 14 September 2023.
4. For example, Paul Kennedy, *The Rise and Fall of the Great Powers: Economic Change and Military Conflict from 1500 to 2000* (Random House USA, 1987).
5. 'Datamapper', *International Monetary Fund 2023* (https://www.imf.org/external/datamapper/NGDP_RPCH@WEO/OEMDC/ADVEC/WEOWORLD).
6. Philip Inman, 'China becomes world's largest exporter', *Guardian*, 10 January 2010.
7. 'Clean Energy Supply Chains Vulnerabilities', in *Energy Technology Perspectives 2023*, International Energy Agency report.
8. 'ASEAN Key Figures 2021', ASEAN Secretariat.
9. 'ASEAN Investment Report 2022', UNCTAD.

10. Mark A. Green, 'China is the Top Trading Partner to More Than 120 Countries', *Wilson Center*, 17 January 2023.

11. Mohamed Al-Sudairi, Steven Jiawei Hai, Kameal Alahmad, 'How Saudi Arabia Bent China to its Techno-Scientific Ambitions', *Carnegie Endowment for International Peace Paper*, 1 August 2023.

12. White House, *National Security Strategy*, October 2022.

13. Aaron L. Friedberg, *Getting China Wrong* (Wiley, 2022).

14. Robert B. Zoellick, 'Whither China? From Membership to Responsibility', *Remarks to National Committee on US–China Relations*, 21 September 2005.

15. 'China Exports by Country', *Trading Economics* (https://tradingeconomics.com/china/exports-by-country).

16. Brad W. Setser, 'China Isn't Shifting Away from the Dollar or Dollar Bonds', *Council of Foreign Relations*, 3 October 2023.

17. Min-hua Chang, 'China More Dependent on US and Our Technology Than You Might Think', *Heritage Foundation*, 7 July 2022.

18. *US Exports to China: Goods and Services Exports to China and the Jobs They Support* (US–China Business Council, 2023).

19. Cheng Li, 'China's Growing Prominence in the Aviation Market and the "Space Club"', *China–US Focus, The Reshuffling Report*, 5 August 2022; 'China Country Guide – Aviation', *International Trade Administration*, US Department of Commerce, 7 April 2023.

20. Steve Holland, Dona Chiacu, 'US and allies accuse China of global hacking spree', Reuters, 20 July 2021.

21. Thilo Hanemann, Mark Witzke, Charlie Vest, Lauren Dudley, Ryan Featherston, 'An Outbound Investment Screening Regime for the United States?', *The Rhodium Group*, January 2022.

22. 'Trends in World Military Expenditure, 2022', *SIPRI Fact Sheet*, April 2023.

23. Sun Yu-ching, William Hetherington, 'China is Upgrading Missiles Targeting Taiwan', *Taipei Times*, 25 July 2023.

24. Tom Wright, Bradley Hope, 'China Offered to Bail Out Troubled Malaysian Fund in Return for Deals', *Wall Street Journal*, 7 January 2019.

25. Some of the best US and Chinese analysts explain why and how the dynamics of the US–China relationship changed in the last few decades in Evan S. Medeiros (ed.), *Cold Rivals: The New Era of US-China Strategic Competition* (Georgetown University Press, 2023).

26. Alex W. Palmer, '"An Act of War": Inside America's Silicon Blockage Against China', *New York Times*, 12 July 2023.

27. Alicia García-Herrero, 'What is behind China's Dual Circulation Strategy?', *China Leadership Monitor*, 1 September 2021.
28. Brad. W. Setser, 'How to Hide Your Foreign Exchange Reserves: A User's Guide', *Council of Foreign Relations*, 29 June 2023.
29. 'China's currency rises in cross-border trade but remains limited globally', *Goldman Sachs Intelligence*, 26 July 2023.

3: America is not all it was

1. Ishaan Tharoor, 'Biden's foreign policy aims to "win the 21st century"', *Washington Post*, 28 April 2021.
2. G. John Ikenberry, 'The end of liberal international order?', *International Affairs*, Vol. 94, No. 1, January 2018.
3. See, for example, Laura Silver, Shannon Schumacher, Mara Mordecai, Shannon Greenwood, Michael Keegan, 'In U.S. and UK, Globalization Leaves Some Feeling "Left Behind" or "Swept Up"', *Pew Research Center*, 5 October 2020.
4. Richard V. Reeves, Katherine Guyot, 'Fewer Americans are making more than their parents did – especially if they grew up in the middle class', *Brookings Commentary*, 25 July 2018.
5. Juliana Menasce Horowitz, Ruth Igielnik, Rakesh Kochhar, 'Trends in Income and Wealth Inequality', *Pew Research Center*, 9 January 2020.
6. Drew Desilver, 'The polarization in today's politics has roots that go back decades', *Pew Research Center*, 10 March 2022.
7. Doug Palmer, 'America's trade gap soared under Trump, final figures show', *Politico*, 5 February 2021.
8. Jake Sullivan, 'Renewing American Economic Leadership', remarks at the Brookings Institution, 27 April 2023 (www.whitehouse.gov).
9. 'Chart Book: Tracking the Recovery from the Pandemic Recession', *Center on Budget and Policy Priorities*, 12 October 2023.
10. 'What's Behind Shocking US Life Expectancy Decline – And What To Do About It', *Harvard T. H. Chan School of Public Health*, 13 April 2023; 'The Employment Situation: September 2023', US Department of Labor, 6 October 2023; Ryan McMaken, 'Why do Americans Have Such High Incomes and Such Low Savings?', *Mises Wire*, 26 August 2016.
11. Aaron Blake, Michael Birnbaum, 'Trump says he threatened not to defend NATO against Russia', *Washington Post*, 22 April 2022.
12. Michael Stott, 'US reluctance on trade deals sends Latin America towards China', *Financial Times*, 24 May 2023.
13. Aidan Arasingham, Emily Benson, 'The IPEF gains momentum but lacks market access', *East Asia Forum*, 30 June 2022.

4: Russia's new ambitions

1. 'Memory and Pride', *Levada Center*, 5 November 2020.
2. Comparative data from UNstats, IMF and World Bank (https://en.wikipedia.org/wiki/List_of_countries_by_largest_historical_GDP).
3. Moira Fagan, Jacob Poushter, Sneha Gubbala, 'Overall opinion of Russia', *Pew Research Center*, 10 July 2023.
4. Emmanuel Macron, 'Closing Speech at the GlobSec Summit, Bratislava', 31 May 2023; Joseph de Weck, 'Why Macron is Now Embracing NATO and EU Enlargement', *Internationale Politik Quarterly*, 29 June 2023.
5. Julian Borger, 'Barack Obama: Russia is a regional power showing weakness over Ukraine', *Guardian*, 25 March 2014.
6. 'Grand Jury Indicts Thirteen Russian Individuals and Three Russian Companies for Scheme to Interfere in the US Political System', US Department of Justice, Office of Public Affairs, 16 February 2018.
7. 'The European Deterrence Initiative: A Budgetary Overview', *Congressional Research Service 'In Focus'*, 1 July 2021.
8. Ian Garner, *Generation Z: Into the Heart of Russia's Fascist Youth* (Hurst, 2023).
9. Sankalp Gurjar, 'Russia–China–South Africa Naval Exercises and Indian Ocean Geopolitics', *Geopolitical Monitor*, 28 February 2023.
10. 'Chinese arms could revive Russia's failing war', *The Economist*, 2 March 2023.
11. 'China-Russia trade hits 218 bln in Jan-Nov, completing goal planned to achieve in 2024', Reuters, 7 December 2023.
12. Gleb Stolyarov, Alexander Marrow, 'Made in Russia? Chinese Cars Drive a Revival of Russia's Auto Factories', Reuters, 20 July 2023.
13. Ailing Tan, 'China's Russia Energy Imports Balloon to $88 billion since War', *Bloomberg*, 21 March 2023.
14. Paul Goble, 'China Helping Russia on Northern Sea Route but Ready to Push Moscow Aside Later', *Eurasia Daily Monitor*, The Jamestown Foundation, 6 May 2021.

5: The ideological roots of the New Cold War

1. For an assessment of the ideological and intellectual debates surrounding Xi Jinping's rise to power, see Rana Mitter, 'China: Cold War or Hot Peace?', *The Critic*, June 2021.

2. Charlotte Gao, 'The CCP Vows to "Lead Everything" Once Again', *The Diplomat*, 28 October 2017.
3. Xi Jinping thought is known formally as 'Xi Jinping Thought on Socialism with Chinese Characteristics for a New Era'. See Kevin Rudd, *The Avoidable War: The Dangers of a Catastrophic Conflict between the US and Xi Jinping's China* (Public Affairs, 2022), pp. 56–8, 88–9.
4. 'China Spends More on Controlling its 1.4 Billion People than on Defence', *Nikkei Asia*, 29 August 2022.
5. See *Russia–China Joint Statement*, 4 February 2022.
6. Larry Diamond, 'A Report Card on Democracy', *Hoover Institution*, 30 July 2000.
7. Alex Vines, Creon Butler, Yu Jie, 'The Response to Debt Distress in Africa and the Role of China', *Chatham House*, 15 December 2022.
8. See, for example, Kerry Brown, *Xi: A Study in Power* (Icon, 2022), p. 120.
9. Emma Graham-Harrison, 'Women pushed even further from power in Xi Jinping's China', *Guardian*, 23 October 2022.
10. Jason Horowitz, 'The Russian Orthodox Leader at the Heart of Putin's Ambitions', *New York Times*, 22 May 2022.
11. Yana Gorokhovoskaia, Adrian Shahbaz, Amy Slipowitz, 'Freedom in the World 2023: Marking 50 Years in the Struggle for Democracy', *Freedom House* (March 2023).

6: A renewed transatlantic partnership

1. 'European Union's Arms Embargo on China: Implications and Options for US Policy', *US Congressional Research Service Report*, 26 January 2006.
2. Thilo Hanemann, Mikko Huotari, 'A New Record Year for Chinese Outbound Investment in Europe', *MERICS and Rhodium Group report*, February 2016.
3. 'Europe was the main destination for US LNG exports in 2022', *US Energy Information Administration*, 22 March 2023.
4. Paul McLeary, Suzanne Lynch, 'The US Wants Europe to Buy American Weapons: The EU Has Other Ideas', *Politico*, 14 June 2023.
5. Jana Puglierin, Pawel Zerka, 'Keeping America close, Russia down, and China far away: How Europeans navigate a competitive world', *European Council on Foreign Relations*, 7 June 2023.
6. Emily Rauhala, 'Macron's Taiwan Comments Anger Allies, Delight Beijing', *Washington Post*, 11 April 2023.

7. Sylvie Bermann, Elvire Fabry, 'Building Europe's Strategic Autonomy vis-à-vis China', *Jacques Delors Institute Working Group Report*, December 2021.
8. *EU–China: A Strategic Outlook*, European Commission, 12 March 2019.
9. *Business Confidence Survey 2023*, The European Union Chamber of Commerce in China.
10. Andy Bounds, Sam Fleming, 'EU trade chief to push China on barriers to exports', *Financial Times*, 7 August 2023.
11. Philip Blenkinsop, 'EU to investigate "flood" of Chinese electric cars, weigh tariffs', Reuters, 13 September 2023.
12. Laura Silver, Christine Huang, Laura Clancy, 'China's Approach to Foreign Policy Gets Largely Negative Reviews in 24 Countries', *Pew Research Center*, 27 July 2023.
13. 'European Council Conclusions on China', *Council of the European Union*, 30 June 2023.
14. '6th European Union–African Union Summit: A Joint Vision for 2030', *European External Action Service*, 17–18 February 2022.
15. 'Keeping America Close, Russia Down, and China Far Away', *European Council on Foreign Relations*, 7 June 2023.
16. *NATO 2022 Strategic Concept*, paragraph 13, 29 June 2022.

7: America's Atlantic and Pacific allies converge

1. 'South Korean Trade in Figures', *Santander Bank, Trade Markets* (https://santandertrade.com/en/portal/analyse-markets/south-korea/foreign-trade-in-figures?url_de_la_page); World's Top Exports (https://www.worldstopexports.com/south-koreas-top-import-partners/?expand_article=1).
2. Kim Young-jin, 'Why Ieodo Matters', *Korea Times*, 18 September 2012.
3. Darren J. Lim, 'Chinese Foreign Economic Coercion during the THAAD Dispute', *Asan Forum*, 28 December 2019.
4. *USNI News*, 18 July 2023.
5. 'China lodges complaint over South Korean president's "erroneous" Taiwan remarks', Reuters, 23 April 2023.
6. Christian Davies, 'Korea battery materials maker onshores China supply chain to win US subsidies', *Financial Times*, 13 August 2023.
7. 'The Spirit of Camp David: Joint Statement of Japan, the Republic of Korea, and the United States', White House, 18 August 2023.
8. 'Are Chinese tourists coming back to Japan?', SuMi Trust, 10 August 2023.

9. 'Japan says Chinese coast guard ships in longest violation of its territorial waters in a decade', CNN, 26 June 2022.
10. Victor Teo, 'Japan's Weapons Transfers to Southeast Asia: Challenges and Opportunities', *ISEAS Yusof Ishak Institute*, 25 May 2021.
11. 'Remarks by President Biden and Prime Minister Kishida Fumio of Japan', Akasaka, Japan, 23 May 2022 (www.whitehouse. gov).
12. Luke Caggiano, 'Japan to Purchase US Tomahawk Missiles', *Arms Control Today*, March 2023.
13. Laura He, 'Australia's exports to China hit record high as relations thaw', CNN, 5 May 2023.
14. Hans Hendrischke, 'Chinese investment in Australia increases for the first time since 2016', *University of Sydney*, 3 May 2023.
15. Peter Jennings, 'Handling of Darwin port lease a fiasco on both sides of politics', *Australian Strategic Policy Institute*, 10 May 2022.
16. Mick Ryan, 'A New Defense Review for Australia', *CSIS*, 27 April 2023.
17. Stephan Haggard, 'South Korea, Ukraine, and Russia: The Economic Dimension', *Korea Economic Institute of America*, 18 May 2022.
18. Akihiro Iwashita, 'Bested by Russia: Abe's Failed Northern Territories Negotiations', *Kennan Cable No. 60, Wilson Center*, November 2020.
19. See Russia Sanctions Tracker, *Ashurst Insights*, 29 August 2023 (https://www.ashurst.com/en/insights/japan-sanctions/).
20. Japan Ministry of Foreign Affairs, 11 January 2023.
21. 'Special address by US Treasury Secretary Janet L. Yellen', *Atlantic Council*, 13 April 2022.
22. Stephen Borowiec, 'Japan Lifts Final South Korea Trade Restriction', *Nikkei Asia*, 27 June 2023.

8: The non-aligned are now the majority and finding their voice

1. Nicholas Lees, 'The Brandt Line After Forty Years', *Review of International Studies*, 18 November 2020.
2. 'How India could rise to the world's second biggest economy', *Goldman Sachs*, 6 July 2023.
3. 'The South–South Trade Partnership', *UN Conference on Trade and Development, Trade Forum 2023*, 8 May 2023.
4. Henry Foy, David Sheppard, 'EU urged to crack down on imports of Indian fuels made with Russian oil', *Financial Times*, 16 May 2023.

5. Pieter D. Wezeman, Justine Gadon, Siemon T. Wezeman, 'Trends in International Arms Transfers, 2022', *Stockholm International Peace Research Institute*, March 2023.
6. Dominique Fraser, 'The Quad: A Backgrounder', *Asia Society Policy Institute*, 16 May 2023.
7. 'Joint Statement from the US and India', *White House Briefing Room*, 22 June 2023 (www.whitehouse.gov).
8. Mohammed Al Sudairi, Steven Jiawei Hai, Kameal Alahmad, 'How Saudi Arabia Bent China to its Technoscientific Ambitions', *Carnegie Endowment for International Peace*, 1 August 2023.
9. Oliver Stuenkel, 'Lula's Foreign Policy: Normalisation and Friction', *Real Instituto Elcano*, 22 June 2023.
10. 'India has more than 800 million internet users', *Indian Express*, 12 December 2022.
11. Rachmi Hertante, 'Between a mineral and a hard place; Indonesia's export ban on raw minerals', *Transnational Institute*, 15 June 2023.
12. Steve Banker, 'Apple's Reliance on China Poses a Problem for the Company', *Forbes*, 19 June 2023.

9: The fight against climate change gets even harder

1. Rebecca Lindsey, 'Climate change: Atmospheric Carbon Dioxide', *National Oceanic and Atmospheric Administration*, 12 May 2023.
2. Gustaf Ekholm, 'On the Variations of the Climate, of the Geological and Historical Past and their Causes', *Quarterly Journal of the Royal Meteorological Society* (1901).
3. *Climate Change 2023: Synthesis Report*, UN Environment Programme, 20 March 2023.
4. For a comprehensive description of how the world is on the edge of its 'ecological limits' see Peter Frankopan, *The Earth Transformed: An Untold History* (Bloomsbury, 2023), pp. 624–34.
5. See 'Principles of Climate Justice', Mary Robinson Foundation (www.mrfcj.org).
6. Zack Colman, 'Kerry's trip to China yields no breakthrough on climate,' *Politico*, 19 July 2023.
7. Data drawn from 'GHG Emissions of All World Countries', *Joint Research Centre, European Commission*, EUR 31658 EN, 2023; and Leandro Vigna, Johannes Friedrich, '9 Charts Explain Per Capita Greenhouse Gas Emissions By Country', *World Resources Institute*, 8 May 2023.
8. Jennifer Scott, 'Rishi Sunak stands by oil drilling expansion as critics warn of climate consequences', *Sky News*, 1 August 2023.

9. Karl Mathiesen, 'China's Xi slams EU carbon border levy plans', *Politico*, 16 April 2021.
10. Federica di Sario, Giorgia Leali, 'Europe takes climate fight global as carbon border tax goes live', *Politico*, 1 October 2023.
11. Report by the OECD Secretary General, 'Climate Finance Provided and Mobilised by Developed Countries in 2013–21' (OECD, 2023).
12. See 'Ukraine Support Tracker', University of Kiel (https://www.ifw-kiel.de/topics/war-against-ukraine/ukraine-support-tracker/).
13. Peter Frankopan, ibid., p. 639.

10: The end of multilateralism

1. 'IMF Members' Quotas and Voting Power', *International Monetary Fund*, accessed 19 October 2023 (https://www.imf.org/en/About/executive-board/members-quotas).
2. *Universal Declaration of Human Rights*, 10 December 1948 (https://www.un.org/sites/un2.un.org/files/2021/03/udhr.pdf).
3. *Universal Declaration of Human Rights, Illustrated Edition*, 2015, UN Regional Information Center, Office of the UN Commission for Human Rights – Regional office for Europe (https://www.un.org/en/udhrbook/pdf/udhr_booklet_en_web.pdf).
4. 'Trump's 2017 UN Speech Transcript', *Politico*, 19 September 2017.
5. Carla Freeman, Alex Stephenson, 'Xi Ramps Up Campaign for a Post-Pax Americana Security Order', *United States Institute of Peace*, 4 May 2023.
6. Courtney J. Fung, Shing-Hon Lam, 'China already leads four of the UN's specialized agencies, and is aiming for a fifth', *Washington Post*, 3 March 2020.
7. Jamey Keaten, 'UN Human Rights Council Rejects Western Bid to Debate China's Xinjiang Abuses', *The Diplomat*, 6 October 2022.
8. Harriet Moynihan, Champa Patel, 'Restrictions on online freedom of expression in China: The domestic, regional and international implications of China's policies and practices', *Chatham House Research Paper*, 17 March 2021.
9. Kataryna Wolczuk, Rilka Dragneva, Jon Wallace, 'What is the Eurasian Economic Union?', *Chatham House Explainer*, 15 July 2022.
10. *A new centre of gravity: the regional comprehensive economic partnership and its trade effects* (United Nations Conference on Trade and Development 2021).

11. *XV BRICS Summit Johannesburg II Declaration*, paragraph 10, 23 August 2023.
12. 'Brics countries launch new development bank in Shanghai', BBC, 21 July 2015 (https://www.bbc.co.uk/news/33605230).
13. Hudson Lockett, Cheng Leng, 'Renminbi's share of trade finance doubles since start of Ukraine war', *Financial Times*, 11 April 2023.
14. Attracta Mooney, Aime Williams, Edward White, 'China accused of using "wrecking tactic" at climate talks', *Financial Times*, 28 July 2023.

11: How to survive and prosper in the New Cold War

1. Frederick Kempe, 'When we are together we drive these changes: What Xi and Putin's deepening alliance means for world order', *Atlantic Council*, 25 March 2023.
2. Yeuw Lun Tian, Ben Blanchard, 'China will never renounce right to use force over Taiwan', Reuters, 16 October 2022.
3. Ian Williams, 'China aims to squeeze life out of Taiwan's chip industry', *The Times* (London), 15 April 2023.
4. See, for example, Zack Cooper, Hal Brands, 'America Will Only Win When China Fails', *Foreign Policy*, 11 March 2021; Michael Mandelbaum, 'The New Containment: Handling Russia, China, Iran', *Foreign Affairs*, March/April 2019.
5. 'Trends in World Military Expenditure 2022', *Stockholm International Peace Research Institute*, April 2023.
6. 'Gross Domestic Spending on R&D', *OECD Data 2023* (https://data.oecd.org/rd/gross-domestic-spending-on-r-d.htm).
7. 'World University Rankings 2023', *Times Higher Education* (https://www.timeshighereducation.com/world-university-rankings/2023/world-ranking).
8. 'World Intellectual Property Indicators 2022', *World Intellectual Property Organization* (2022).
9. This was the reasoning behind the prescient proposal by Ivo Daalder and Jim Lindsay in 2018 to create a G9 *excluding* the Trump-led US, but including the EU alongside Australia, South Korea and all the other G7 members. 'The Committee to Save the World Order: America's Allies Must Step Up as America Steps Down', *Foreign Affairs*, November/December 2018.
10. Jake Sullivan, 'Renewing American Leadership', *Brookings Institution*, 27 April 2023.
11. 'Remarks by Jake Sullivan at the Special Competitive Strategies Project Global Emerging Technologies Summit', 16 September 2022 (www.whitehouse.gov).

12. Shoichiro Taguchi, 'US considering curbing China's cloud access, US official says', *Nikkei Asia*, 21 October 2023.

13. Allen Rappeport, 'A Rural Michigan Town Is the Latest Battleground in the US–China Fight', *New York Times*, 3 October 2023.

14. *America's Strategic Posture: The Final Report of the Commission on the Strategic Posture of the United States*, Madelyn R. Creedon (Chair), Jon L. Kyl (Vice Chair), October 2023.

15. This risk has been highlighted by Lawrence Freedman, *The Future of War: A History* (Allen Lane, 2017), pp. 281–2; and more recently by Ed Luce, 'The world cannot hedge against Donald Trump', *Financial Times*, 7 December 2023.

16. Leslie Vinjamuri, 'Why Multilateralism Still Matters: The Way to Win Over the Global South', *Foreign Affairs*, 2 October 2023.

17. *Fact Sheet: President Biden and Prime Minister Modi Host Leaders on the Global Partnership for Infrastructure and Investment*, 9 September 2023 (www.whitehouse.gov).

18. 'AIIB President Jin Liqun Meets With World Bank President Nominee Ajay Banga', *AIIB*, 22 March 2023.

19. 'The AIIB and IBRD to Establish New Guarantee Facility to Address G20 Capital Adequacy Framework Recommendations', *AIIB*, 23 June 2023.

Conclusion

1. Kevin Rudd, ibid.

2. 'Donald Trump's second term would be a protectionist nightmare', *The Economist*, 31 October 2023.

ACKNOWLEDGEMENTS

This book has its genesis in a moment of serendipity in early 2023, when I was introduced to Publisher Poppy Hampson. She encouraged me to weave together the threads of the big changes in international relations that I observed during my time at Chatham House, when the period of hope that followed the end of the Cold War gave way to the geopolitical division and widespread violence that we witness today. But I am a Gramscian at heart – whatever the pessimism of the mind, I believe in the optimism of the will, and, as I note in the book, there is much that is potentially positive about the future, especially if we can lift our sights from the risks of the New Cold War to the opportunities in the Global South.

I am deeply grateful to my colleagues at Chatham House, CSIS, the Asia Society and other think tanks and academic institutions, who bring shape to the seeming chaos of international relations. I am equally grateful to those policy practitioners who help by confidentially sharing their experience with us. I want to thank Poppy and the whole team at Atlantic Books, especially Harry O'Sullivan, for their comments and suggestions on the early drafts, and to John English for his copy-editing. I have also greatly appreciated the wisdom and guidance offered by my agent, Natasha Fairweather.

This book is dedicated to my life and soul partner Trisha de Borchgrave, who never ceases to offer me intellectual challenge and substantive companionship, and to our two wonderful daughters, Marina and Saskia.

INDEX